To Kath

for your special birthday!

Much love

Helen
xxxx

La Vita è Bella

La Vita è Bella

The elegant art of living
in the Italian style

Jill Foulston

RYLAND PETERS & SMALL
LONDON • NEW YORK

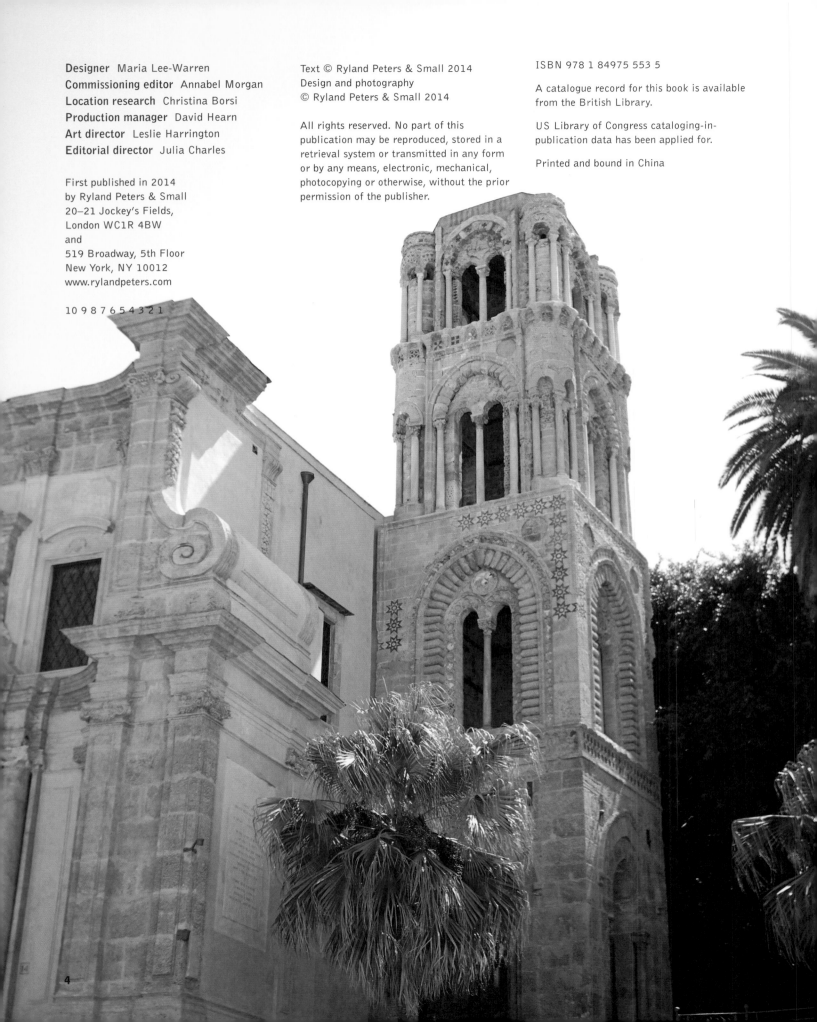

Designer Maria Lee-Warren
Commissioning editor Annabel Morgan
Location research Christina Borsi
Production manager David Hearn
Art director Leslie Harrington
Editorial director Julia Charles

First published in 2014
by Ryland Peters & Small
20–21 Jockey's Fields,
London WC1R 4BW
and
519 Broadway, 5th Floor
New York, NY 10012
www.rylandpeters.com

10 9 8 7 6 5 4 3 2 1

Text © Ryland Peters & Small 2014
Design and photography
© Ryland Peters & Small 2014

ISBN 978 1 84975 553 5

A catalogue record for this book is available
from the British Library.

US Library of Congress cataloging-in-
publication data has been applied for.

Printed and bound in China

4

Contents

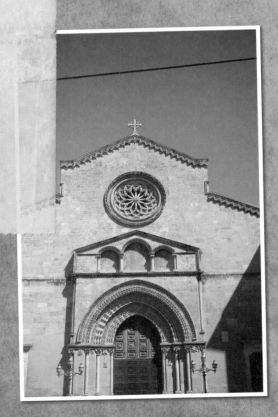

Antica Focacceria S. Francesco

1834

Introduction

Like so many northerners before me, I crossed the Alps and fell completely in love with Italy. I made the initial trip as a child. We'd come from Switzerland to the lakes, and I remember vividly my first sight of Lake Maggiore, with Isola Bella rising up out of the mist like a mirage.

From that time on, no matter the virtues of other travel destinations, it was to Italy that I always wanted to return – for the sunniness of its people, the beauty of its landscapes and its incredible cities. From a base in Umbria, further visits have gradually taken me deeper into the south and on to Sicily. The country's complicated history has resulted in a rich layering of culture that's reflected in its food and buildings, even its language. And although no one can afford to miss the magic of Rome, Florence, Venice and Milan, it is just as rewarding to visit out-of-the-way places, such as the northern town of Sabbioneta, where classical gods and goddesses look down on you in the Renaissance *Teatro all'antica*, or Pitigliano, in southern Tuscany, where the Jewish population once baked their matzoh bread in a cave.

Italians often prefer to holiday in their own country, and it's easy to understand why. Like everyone else, they also love travelling outside of it, of course. But in a land that extends from the Alps almost to Africa, it really is possible to be continually surprised by the landscape and regional customs.

La Vita è Bella celebrates Italy's surprises, its past and its present. Focusing on four well-loved regions, it moves from the beauty of the lakes in the north through the gentle heartland of Tuscany and Umbria. Plunging headfirst into Rome's glorious chaos and then meandering down the breathtaking Amalfi Coast, it ventures into the wilder landscape of the extreme south before hopping across the Strait of Messina to Sicily, where a succession of occupying powers – Arabic, Greek, Norman and Spanish – have left their marks on a complex culture.

Each chapter in this book explores Italy through its food, customs and architecture. Mouthwatering recipes highlight traditional dishes from the four regions, and there are visits to Italian gardens and *caffès*, olive oil and *gelato* tasting, a look at Italian cinema, Sicilian sweets, opera and more.

The chapters also open the door to 15 individual homes. There's an ivy-clad waterside tower house on Lake Como with an industrial aesthetic; a converted Tuscan farmhouse boasting its own chapel; an exotic 18th-century merchant's house on the Amalfi Coast and a mysterious cave house in Modica in Sicily. Through careful borrowing from the past, each owner has designed a home for contemporary living, with an eye to the future.

Il Nord

The North – Milan,
Turin and the Lakes

Vini e Liquori

Italy's unique geography and climate allows for grapes to be cultivated from the Alps in the north all the way down to the southernmost tip of the peninsula. There are 20 designated wine-growing regions and over 350 documented, authorized varietals, in addition to four basic categories of recognized wines. ·

Vini are local wines made from any sort of grape, while *vini varietali* contain approximately 85% of an authorized grape variety. Both these categories may come from anywhere in the EU. *Vini IGP* (Wines with Protected Geographical Indication) are produced in a specific territory within Italy and conform to certain specifications. The most highly prized wines are those with the DOP and DOCG status. These are produced in smaller, established wine-making territories and following stricter production regulations. They must also pass a rigorous tasting committee.

Italians generally drink their liquori in moderation, enjoying them with meals or in a morning coffee.

Italians generally drink their *liquori* in moderation, enjoying them with meals and occasionally in a morning coffee. Served before dinner, an *aperitivo* stimulates the appetite. It is commonly non-alcoholic, like Sanbittèr, or very bitter, a taste relished by Italians. You might try Amaretto ('a little bitter'), Campari, Cynar (curiously, made from artichokes), Fernet-Branca, originally marketed as a medicine, or Strega, meaning 'witch'. And, of course, there's Martini, the base of the world-famous cocktail.

After dinner, you may be offered Frangelico, a sweet *liquore* made with hazelnuts; *grappa*, a popular type of brandy made from the peels, seeds and stems of grapes; *limoncello*, the gloriously lemony drink from the Amalfi Coast; rich, port-like *Marsala*; *sambuca*, made from star anise and elderflowers, or *Vin Santo*, a sweet 'holy' wine served with *cantucci* biscuits.

-The rich cuisine of northern Italy makes use of the exceptional dairy products from cattle raised in the Emilia-Romagna region. Unsalted butter is called for more commonly than olive oil, and saffron, which is grown in the north as well as throughout the rest of the country, is indispensable. The base of this dish is, of course, rice, whose cultivation in Italy probably began in the Renaissance: it was mentioned in a letter written by the Duke of Milan, who around 1475 sent a sack to the Duke of Ferrara and advised him to cultivate it. The fertile plains near Milan are perfectly suited to growing the grain, and the firm bite and creaminess of arborio or carnaroli rice are ideal for this *risotto*. It is often served as the first course in a meal that includes *ossobuco* (see pages 26–27).

Risotto Milanese

1 litre/quart good-quality chicken stock, heated until just boiling
a good pinch saffron threads
50 g/½ stick butter, plus extra to serve
1 onion, finely chopped
25 g/1 oz. beef marrow (optional)
300 g/1½ cups *risotto* rice, preferably arborio
100 ml/½ cup Italian dry white wine
25 g/¼ cup freshly grated Parmesan cheese, plus extra to serve
sea salt and freshly ground black pepper

Serves 2

Place the stock in a saucepan and bring to a gentle simmer. Pound the saffron strands in a pestle and mortar to make a powder and place in a small bowl. Add about 100 ml/½ cup of the stock and set aside to infuse.

Melt half the butter in a saucepan and gently fry the onion and marrow, if using, with a little salt and pepper over a medium–low heat for 10 minutes until really soft but not browned. Add the rice and stir for about 1 minute until all the grains appear glossy.

Add the wine and simmer for 2–3 minutes until it is almost all evaporated. Gradually start adding the gently simmering stock about 200 ml/1 cup at a time, stirring the rice constantly with a wooden spoon, allowing the rice to absorb most of the stock before adding more. Continue this for about 20 minutes until the rice is *al dente* and the stock all but absorbed.

Strain in the saffron-infused stock, the remaining butter and the Parmesan, and serve as soon as the cheese is melted.

Always serve the risotto with extra cheese and butter.

beautiful country in the world ... that
others must stand off and be hushed
while she speaks.

Henry James

Italy is really so much the most beautiful country in the world ... that others must stand off and be hushed while she speaks. Henry James

THIS PAGE AND OPPOSITE
This apartment underwent a fairly radical transformation, yet it retains traces of the 19th-century Liberty style, including the elegant stucco rosette on the living-room ceiling and a bow window that fills the room with light. Carlotta designs and produces exotic and brightly coloured one-off pieces for her very successful brand, L'Officina dell'Invisibile, using skilled craftsmen in Brazil and Italy. Every item in her line, whether cushion, sofa, bedding or jewellery, is cheerful and full of personality. In the living room (opposite), warm tones of rust, cherry and aubergine are set against bright white walls, and the industrial look is banished.

The House of the Invisible

In 2005, Carlotta Oddone decided to bring her career and home together under one roof. After working as a journalist for 15 years, she wanted to dedicate herself to her real passion: designing interiors and creating objects in the artisan tradition. It was a bold move, since her home town of Turin is rooted in industry, and famous as the manufacturing seat of the Fiat motorcar. Yet nothing could be further removed from the minimalist or industrial style than Carlotta's taste.

First and foremost, Carlotta wanted to find the right home for herself and her children, yet just as important was a showroom for L'Officina dell'Invisibile, her design company – in other words, a space that could easily accommodate both sides of her life. While she was busy searching for somewhere with a huge terrace and a view of the mountains, she stumbled instead across an apartment with a courtyard garden – a rarity in the city centre. 'I had no doubts about it,' Carlotta says. 'It was the home of my dreams.' The property even included a little garden house. 'What more could I have asked for?'

So in February 2005, Carlotta bought this apartment – the first floor of a *palazzo* built in the first decade of the 19th century. However, before the family could move in, it had to undergo 'a fairly radical transformation'. At the time of purchase, the apartment was an office with a long central corridor and small rooms branching off it. Original walls were knocked down to make way for a large kitchen, now the core of the home, and an open-plan living room. To give continuity to the overall space and to bring light from the garden into the rest of the house, large-paned windows were set into the internal walls.

For Carlotta, the kitchen was one of the great successes of the restoration. Neither traditional nor contemporary, it was invented 'piece by piece', without fitted cabinets. Instead, there's a large wardrobe, made to Carlotta's design in Indonesia from bleached, recycled wood, and a table bought second-hand. Only the dishwasher is built in, under a custom-made work surface of Carrara marble. The dining table was also made to her design in stainless steel; surrounding it are iron chairs from Morocco. French doors open onto the terrace, which faces the courtyard garden.

The living room retains some original architectural details, including stucco ceiling mouldings and a bow window that lets in 'a river of light'. Warm and welcoming, it's full of Carlotta's soft furnishings and textiles in an exotic fruit salad of colours: aubergine, paprika and cerise. Thanks to the high ceilings, the walls are the perfect backdrop for hanging rugs and other pieces bought on her world travels. For Carlotta, 'A house doesn't have to be luxurious in order to be beautiful.' Instead, it should exude the personality of the people who live in it.

If there are only two bedrooms in this multi-tasking house, there are many nooks and crannies in which to relax. The space in the boys' bedroom was doubled by creating a sleeping loft, where they read or sleep; below, they study or chat with friends. In the master bedroom, a series of niches carved out of the old chimney flue serve as shelves and nightstands. Again, French doors lead out onto the terrace, where stairs run down to the garden. It was very neglected when Carlotta bought the house. But she closed her eyes and imagined it blooming, with her children running after a ball. Now she can keep her eyes open.

OPPOSITE Light pours through tall French doors into the living room, whose 4-metre-/13-feet-high walls, coloured with natural pigments and water-based enamels, contribute a real sense of space. A photograph of Maimuna hangs behind the sofas. The cushions are upholstered in fabrics designed by Carlotta's firm, and carpets cover the wooden floors.

RIGHT AND ABOVE RIGHT In the master bedroom, a half-wall separates the bed from two sinks and a shower positioned next to the terrace. From the terrace, stairs lead down to Carlotta's studio, which stands in a garden with an old stone fountain in the centre and enormous jasmine plants scenting the air.

Pasta Perfect

It's no surprise that pasta is the world's most popular dish. Italians consume around 27 kilos/60 pounds per person each year, and even allowing for regional variations, there are estimated to be as many as 600 different shapes, ranging from *agnolotti* ('little angels', or soft, pillowy pockets) to *strozzapreti* ('priest-stranglers') and *ziti* ('bridegrooms'). The names are always plural — you wouldn't want to eat only one *spaghetto*, or 'little string' — and suffixes tell you whether the shape is big (*-oni*, as in *cannelloni*, or 'big tubes'), small (*-elle*, as in *tagliatelle*) or ill-made (*-acci*, as in *cappellacci*, 'funny little hats').

Some say it was Marco Polo who brought pasta back to Italy in 1295 from his voyages in China, but in fact the history of pasta in Italy can be traced to at least the first century AD, when the Etrusco-Roman people were making and eating *lagane*, a foodstuff similar to our lasagne, though it was baked rather than boiled.

Something closer to what we'd recognize as pasta — a type of dried noodle product made from durum wheat — arrived in Sicily with the eighth-century Arab invasions, and the first mention of the dish comes in 1154, in a reference to the export of pasta from there. Spreading from the island onto the mainland, manufacture took off in Naples, where there were some 60 pasta shops in 1700. By 1785, that figure had grown to 280.

These days, Italian pasta production is highly regulated, and dried pasta must contain at least some *semola di grano duro*, or durum wheat semolina.

Ossobuco (a bone with a hole in it) first appeared on the menu of an *osteria* (inn or tavern) in a Milan side street in the 19th century and was thought to be a favourite dish of local farmers. To make it, veal shanks cut across the bone are stewed with white wine and a *soffrito*, a lightly braised mixture of onions and other vegetables. It is traditionally accompanied by *gremolata*, a sharp and refreshing sauce of parsley, lemon and garlic, and often served with *Risotto Milanese* (see pages 14–15).

Ossobuco

1.5 kg/3¼ lb. veal shin or
  ossobuco (4 large or
  8 small pieces)
50 g/½ stick butter
1 onion, finely chopped
2 carrots, finely chopped
2 celery stalks, finely
  chopped
2 large garlic cloves,
  crushed
150 ml/⅔ cup Italian dry
  white wine
500 ml/2 cups Italian sieved
  tomato *passata*
250 ml/1 cup beef stock
2 bay leaves, bashed
sea salt and finely ground
  black pepper

Gremolata
grated zest 1 lemon
1 garlic clove, crushed
4 tablespoons chopped fresh
  flat-leaf parsley

1 quantity *Risotto Milanese*,
  to serve (see pages
  14–15)

Serves 4

Take the veal shin (carefully remove the marrow from one of the bones to use in the *risotto*, if wished) and season with salt and pepper. Melt the butter in a large non-stick casserole dish and as soon as it stops foaming fry the veal, in batches, for 5 minutes, or until evenly browned. Remove with a slotted spoon and set aside.

Add the onion, carrots, celery and garlic to the pan and fry gently for 10 minutes until soft and golden. Add the wine and boil for 1 minute, then return the veal to the pan with the tomato *passata*, stock and bay leaves. Bring to the boil, cover with a tight-fitting lid and simmer very gently for 1½–2 hours or until the meat starts to melt from the bone.

Make the *gremolata*. Combine the lemon zest, garlic and parsley, then serve with the *ossobuco* and the *Risotto Milanese*.

The Old Mill

What could be more idyllic than to swim or row across the river for your morning espresso? That's exactly what furniture designer Katrin Arens has done ever since she bought her idyllic farmhouse near Lake Como in the far north of Italy. Katrin came to the area from Düsseldorf, Germany, after winning a scholarship at the Academy of Arts in Bergamo, and the furniture business that she started then is still going strong.

ABOVE AND ABOVE RIGHT Open shelving highlights the simplicity of the utensils: an aluminium teapot, Moka coffee-makers and wooden spoons. Each of the nine compartments in an upright pallet contains colourful pottery held in place with bent nails.

RIGHT Katrin's kitchen shows the transforming powers of her design aesthetic: reuse, recycle, re-love. Cupboard doors were made from old shutters and the original cement floor was left bare and complemented by a cement work surface.

THIS PAGE Upstairs are two tall, narrow bookcases with graduated tops that look almost sculptural. They blend in with the white walls of what was formerly a monastery and mill house. The only colour comes from an evocative oil painting next to them by Hella Arens, Katrin's mother, and blown-glass objects in cheerful pastels.

OPPOSITE A teak and rattan chaise-longue from Sri Lanka is strategically placed next to the wood-burning stove. Rather than installing central heating in the house, Katrin instead burns castoffs and scraps from her furniture production to warm the interior. The graceful arched window provides ample light for reading.

When she discovered the house, Katrin was pregnant. She and her boyfriend had been searching for a place that would accommodate life and work, and they found it in the village of Pontida on the river Adda. This former monastery and mill was the right size for both a family and a business.

The house had been empty for nearly ten years and was without electricity, heating or hot water. Katrin set up her furniture business on the ground floor while the couple lived on the first floor and started renovating the building, which was in very poor condition. Some windows had been bricked up, while others were open to the sky, allowing the

swallows the freedom of the house. 'We left one window open until the end of that summer, when the last birds in the nest had learned to fly outside.' The one nest they preserved in the ceiling beams can still be seen there today.

Walls and ceilings that were dark brown and green before renovation were painted pure white. The original cement floors were preserved in some rooms, and others were painted. Katrin made new doors from old shutters and created a kitchen with a cement work surface. That kitchen is where they now gather, Katrin to cook and her children, Laura, 15, and Sofia, 8, to do their homework.

THIS PAGE Katrin's interiors are simple and elegant, accented only by pieces she collects when travelling and her own furniture designs. In the bedrooms, the doors are of unpainted wood with unusual, geometric wooden latches. Beds are covered in natural cotton and linen in neutral colours. The simplicity of the interiors recalls the building's monastic past.

THIS PAGE A small square nightstand echoes the straight, uncomplicated lines of the monumental four-poster bed beside it. Natural linen provides the drapery over the bed. In the kitchen, an old rake makes the perfect towel rack. Every piece in this house tells a story, and Katrin loves giving fresh significance to previously unloved materials by turning them into something new and useful.

None of the original monastic simplicity has been lost. There is still no central heating. Instead, wood pellets heat part of the house and wooden offcuts from the furniture production are burned in the kitchen stove. The family keep fit lugging wood up to the first floor every day.

Since the beginning, Katrin's goal has been to realize simple yet elegant functional objects. It's a formula that works. Throughout the airy spaces of this eco-haven, old furniture mingles with pieces designed and built by Katrin from reclaimed wood. Katrin loves travelling and often brings inspiration home, whether in the form of local fleamarket finds or larger items from the countries she visits. Asia and South America are especially rewarding hunting grounds. In recent years, Katrin has specialized in designing kitchens with cement or wood work surfaces accented with wooden or iron doors. Her own home breathes light and texture, with gilt mirrors and oil paintings by her mother, Hella Arens, opening up the white spaces still further.

The mill's stunning position, between the river Adda on one side and the mountains on the other, has not been without drawbacks. 'The first few years, the river flooded twice a year, so we had to put everything up high, including the machinery used to make the furniture.' When the river was in full spate, they could only get out of the house by boat. An old spinning mill has since come to the rescue, and production and showroom are now high and dry only minutes away, in the village of Villa d'Adda.

Va-Voom Vespa

When Audrey Hepburn clambered onto Gregory Peck's scooter in the 1953 film *Roman Holiday*, Vespa sales rocketed – and the world fell in love. Not only with Hepburn, but also with the humble motor scooter.

A triumph of Italian manufacturing, the Vespa is the perfect marriage of form and function. It was created after the Second World War, when Italy's economy had taken a battering and the country lacked the funds to reinvest in its automobile industry. People needed a convenient and economical mode of transport, so Enrico Piaggio of the Piaggio aircraft manufacturers contacted the aeronautical engineer Corradino d'Ascanio and asked him to design a practical, affordable vehicle for the general population.

D'Ascanio's 1944 prototype eliminated all the things he hated about motorcycles – dirtiness and unreliability – enclosing the motor and chain beneath a revolutionary solid central body part. When he caught sight of the now iconic design, Piaggio exclaimed '*Sembra una vespa!*' – 'It looks like a wasp!' The first commercial models appeared in 1946, the same year the design was patented. In the 1950s, space was opened up between the seat and the shield, allowing women in skirts to ride the scooter with complete modesty.

The Vespa is still clean, economical to run and small enough to weave in and out of slow-moving traffic. It has the edge over the bulkier, more costly motorcycle, and with its timeless, pastel palette, it epitomizes a fun, carefree lifestyle. No wonder its cheerful buzzing can be heard throughout towns and cities across Italy, as well as the rest of the world.

LEFT AND BELOW This former *casa colonica* (farmhouse) is painted in a faded red accented with green shutters, a colour scheme that's typical of the Alpine region. The cut-outs on the wooden balcony surround are a reminder that this region of Italy, the Veneto, is very close to Austria. Paola looks after the garden herself.

OPPOSITE The warm tones of the terracotta floors in the entrance are in complete harmony with the colours of the walls, on which Paola has painted a decorative design inspired by Fortuny fabrics. The elegant wooden divan is 18th-century Venetian. An open door allows a peek into the kitchen.

Mountain Hideaway

Paola Angoletta spends her holidays in a typical farmhouse, or *casa colonica*, perched on a rocky outcrop above the Piave River in a hamlet in the Veneto. There was a time when the house thrummed to the sound of her extended family; the summers were long and lively, with many of the *contadini* and their animals joining in the happy confusion.

Since inheriting the house from her mother, Paola has worked hard on this *nobildonna*, or great lady, from the 1700s, maintaining or replicating her gorgeous original features. She has consolidated the house's structure, employing traditional building materials and methods, and deliberately evokes the flavour of past times through her choice of decoration and colours — in particular, the rich, faded red of the exterior.

ABOVE The two stately armchairs positioned at the end of the table are 18th-century Venetian.

RIGHT Following period designs, Paola painted dark decorative borders against oatmeal-coloured walls in the dining room as well as in the upstairs bedrooms. The large painting is 17th-century Flemish.

ABOVE On the dining-room table, a kilim is used as a tablecloth. Overhead, an 18th-century Venetian chandelier drips with delicate blue and red flowers. Shelves set into the walls hold large pottery dishes, while family plates are hung decoratively.

The house is a three-storey rectangle with the shingle roof and green-painted shutters that are native to Italian Alpine architecture. Its short side faces south, while the longer side is attached to the agricultural buildings in such a way as to form an 'L' and so protect the courtyard from the strong seasonal winds. Low hedges and pathways bordered by ancient stone walls form natural boundaries to the property and lead deep into the surrounding woods. Once a working farm, the farmhouse still enjoys a splendid view of the entire valley and the towering Dolomites.

As a designer, Paola's customary approach is to 'feel' a house and imagine what it might be. In this case, of course, she had plenty of her own history and experience to guide her. Inside, she has rediscovered original frescoes and some of the old colours. But she's also created new colours, dabbing them over a thin base of whitewash. It's a technique that results in what Paola calls 'timeless' walls, which seem to vibrate with their own energy. Their appearance changes with the light, and sometimes they resemble old velvet. The effect is quite magical.

ABOVE Copper pots march in an orderly fashion across pink walls created by dabbing fresh tint over a base of whitewash to give a velvety effect. The prints below contribute to a pleasingly eclectic tableau.
FAR LEFT AND LEFT A portrait hangs over the original stone fireplace in the living room; almost out of sight is a crystal chandelier. The decorative borders were painted by Paola.
OPPOSITE Paola's house is furnished with family heirlooms. In a corner of the living room, a Venetian lamp from a gondola takes over when the light fades from behind the French doors.

40

The enchantment continues in the garden. Over the years, Paola has looked after it herself, encouraging a rustic but delicate planting with roses, peonies and hydrangeas. In the spring, a 100-year-old wisteria seems part of the old house. Because the winters can be bitter, she has researched resistant species to find hardy flowers that will endure.

Cold winters are one reason the house isn't lived in year-round, as there is no central heating. Instead, there is a huge Larin fireplace in the dining room, the oldest part of the house. Open on two sides, it occupies the centre of the room and is encircled by benches. The floors on this level are of wood or terracotta, and the walls pick up their earthy tones to provide a reddish-orange backdrop for Paola's painting of foliage, inspired by Fortuny fabrics. Such reds, oranges and yellows are traditional tones in the houses of the Veneto. The decorative borders on this floor's walls and in the upstairs bedrooms were also painted by Paola following period designs. Perhaps her most elaborate work

can be found in the upstairs bathroom, whose walls bloom with trompe l'oeil flowered fabric. It's a room that has hardly seen any other intervention, and whose bare beams allow the clawfoot tub and painted wall to take centre stage.

Some of Paola's furniture has come from trips to India, the Orient or markets closer to home. Other pieces are family heirlooms. A second-floor studio hosts books, photos and 19th-century objects from the office of her grandfather, a lawyer. Using this eclectic palette, ensembles have been arranged to form scenes of cosy elegance.

If you look east from the gardens behind the house, you can see the campanile at nearby Belluno and the distant mountains beyond. Paola still summers in the house she has always adored, recreating the family atmosphere of former times by inviting as many friends as possible to sit around the long tables in the courtyard behind it. At long suppers and joyous celebrations in this extraordinary place, the positive energy enables life to be lived to the full.

OPPOSITE A Suzani dress picks up the rich magenta of the banister and Paola's decorative ceiling border in the stairwell; even the risers of the steps blend in, the whole set off beautifully by walls of pale lilac. When things get too serious, this 19th-century ancestor can look down on a white coral bookended by two bouquets of small shells crowned with lacy dark coral. A 19th-century étagère lends support.

THIS PAGE During renovation, Paola discovered original frescoes and old colours on the walls of her family home, including this particularly detailed one in a bedroom (above right). In the bathroom (left), grey borders stretch round the room, and the ancient beams have been left bare; the terracotta floors are partially covered with rugs. Behind the clawfoot bathtub in a midnight blue is Paola's most detailed decorative painting in the house: a trompe l'oeil pattern of flowered fabric.

Panna cotta, or 'cooked cream' is all about the wobble. Beware of indifferent versions – some of the packet mixes available, for example. This one is really good. This dessert is served throughout Italy, and it probably originated in Piedmont or Lombardy, which are known for their rich milk and cream.

Panna Cotta with Orange Zest

500 ml/2 cups double/heavy
   cream
300 ml/1¼ cups milk
1 vanilla pod, split
50 g/¼ cup granulated
   sugar
3 leaves of gelatine or
   3 teaspoons powdered
   gelatine

candied orange zest
2 unwaxed oranges
50 g/¼ cup caster sugar

6 moulds, about 100 ml/
   ½ cup each

Serves 6

To make the *panna cotta*, put the cream and milk, split vanilla pod and granulated sugar in a saucepan and bring to the boil. Crumble or sprinkle the gelatine into the cream mixture and stir until dissolved. Cool, then chill in the refrigerator until it JUST begins to thicken. At this stage, stir the mixture briskly to distribute the vanilla seeds, then remove the vanilla pod. (Rinse and dry, then keep in the sugar jar to flavour.) Pour into the moulds, set on a tray and refrigerate for at least 5 hours or until set.

Remove the zest from the oranges with a sharp potato peeler (removing any bitter white pith with a knife afterwards). Cut the zest into long, fine shreds. Bring a small saucepan of water to the boil and blanch the shreds for 1 minute. Drain, then refresh in cold water.

Put the caster sugar and 100 ml/½ cup water in a small saucepan and stir until dissolved. Add the orange shreds and bring to a rolling boil. Boil for 2–3 minutes, then strain the shreds through a sieve and transfer to a plate to cool. Before they cool too much, separate them out a little so that they don't stick together.

To serve, press the top of the panna cotta and gently pull away from the edge of the mould (this breaks the airlock). Carefully invert onto a small cold plate. Give it a good shake and the panna cotta should simply drop out. If it won't turn out, dip the mould very briefly into warm water, then invert onto the plate again and lift off. Be warned that the panna cotta will melt if the dipping water is too hot. Repeat with the remaining moulds.

Top with the orange shreds and a spoonful of syrup.

Coffee Culture

It's impossible to imagine Italy without coffee. The beverage was introduced to the country through 16th-century trade between Venice and the East, and the first *caffè*, named after its product, opened in Venice in 1683.

Strange as it may seem, coffee was originally considered a suspicious substance. With its Eastern origins, it was viewed as an Islamic threat to Christianity, and Vatican officials begged Pope Clement VIII to prohibit its use. But the pope insisted on trying it first, and when he did, he declared: 'This Satan's drink is delicious…it would be a pity to let the infidels have exclusive use of it. We shall fool Satan by baptizing it.' And he did, in 1600. Or so the story goes.

Italians tend to enjoy their coffee strong and aromatic. Traditional preparation methods force water through tightly packed grounds, and no household is without its *macchinetta*, or simple stovetop coffee-maker. Most Italians also tend to frequent one bar, or *caffè*, which they may visit at any time of the day. Apart from *caffè*, or *espresso*, the most popular types are *caffè latte* (with milk), *caffè corretto* ('corrected' with a shot of grappa), *caffè macchiato* ('marked' or dotted with steamed or cold milk) and *cappuccino*, sometimes called *cappuccio* for short.

Bicerin ('small glass' in local dialect) is a special coffee drink from Turin. Popular since the 18th century, it was praised by Alexandre Dumas in 1852. It's a layered drink of *espresso*, thick hot chocolate and whole milk or cream, served in a glass rather than a cup.

Strange as it may seem, coffee was originally considered a suspicious substance. With its Eastern origins, it was viewed as an Islamic threat to Christianity.

The rain was coming down
in what seemed solid sheets.
But it was Italy. Nothing
it did could be bad.

Elizabeth von Arnim

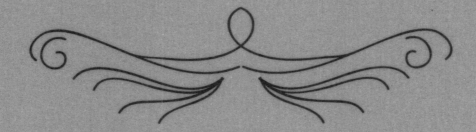

The rain was coming down
in what seemed solid sheets.

Elizabeth von Arnim

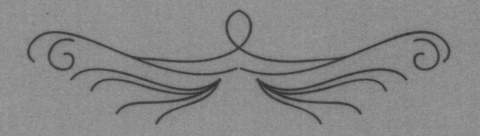

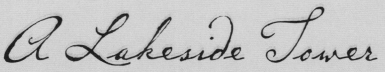

LEFT AND BELOW Fittingly, considering its proximity to Milan, Pietro's lake house has a designer cloak of Canadian ivy to glam up its ancient frame. The 100-year-old plant was one of the factors that influenced Pietro to buy the house; it changes colours with the seasons, becoming bright red in the autumn. A dark green tunnel leads down to the pier and boats (below).

OPPOSITE Pescallo is furnished with an inspiring mixture of the modern – from Pietro's family furniture business – and the rustic. On this terrace, an iron table with weathered wooden planks is surrounded by chairs of the same material in a classic design. The ivy makes music with the lakeside breezes.

A Lakeside Tower

First there were nuns. Then came the fishermen, a photographer, an astronomer…and now, this imposing old house overlooking the serene waters of Lake Como is home to designer Pietro Castagna. Pietro has always been hopelessly in love with the little lakeside town of Bellagio, so it's helpful that his family furniture business is located only an hour away in Milan, making it easy for him to steal away and spend his weekends at this tranquil, enchanted spot on Lake Como.

It could be Pescallo's history as a convent that makes it such a peaceful spot, but it must also be due in no small part to the clean white space Pietro has created, and the pared-back monochrome furnishings. His ambition was to take away, rather than to add, and the simple, uncomplicated style throughout the house reflects those goals. Pietro wanted the space to be calm and uncluttered so that the house's glorious lakeside setting and glossy cloak of ivy would provide the magic.

When Pietro first discovered the house in 2008, it was in a deplorable condition. There was no central heating, no electricity and no plumbing. But it did have a glorious, richly coloured, 100-year-old Canadian ivy draped gracefully over its exterior – to some extent, holding it together. Undeterred, Pietro set about consolidating the building, stabilizing it and making a few necessary structural changes before dividing it up into four units.

Restoring the house was a massive project, as it extends to a vast 600 square metres/6450 square feet. The oldest

LEFT AND ABOVE Books do furnish this room, which wouldn't be complete without Pietro's two Jack Russell terriers. The monochrome scheme throughout contributes to a feeling of comfort and relaxation. Paintings and photographs hang low on the walls or rest directly on the floor in imaginative groupings.

OPPOSITE Floors at the ground level are beaten cement, once used on factory floors around the lake. Most of the furniture in the house, including these white sofas, comes from the family firm in Milan. Shells from Pietro's travels and market finds add texture to his interiors.

part of the structure dates from 1500, and it was enlarged at some point in the 1700s, then again in the 19th century. The tower attached to it was once used to keep watch on the movements of local fishermen so that they could be appropriately taxed. Now, that same tower is home to five of the ten bedrooms in the house.

Pietro shares two of the four units in the house with a friend, and lets the other units to tourists; separate entrances guarantee privacy. There are four kitchens in all, and the largest, quasi-industrial one on the ground floor is Pietro's.

It's where he does the cooking he loves for large groups of friends and family. The remaining kitchens are small but functional, each one stocked with all the appropriate equipment from the family business.

Pietro's own personal part of Pescallo is entered at ground level through the garden, beyond the wine cellars and storerooms. Bookshelves line a spacious, high-ceilinged living room dotted with plump white sofas. Colours here, as elsewhere in the house, are predominantly white, with soft charcoal and subtle beige accents. Light pours through the

ABOVE The horizontally laid planks of the dining table line up with the steps leading upstairs to the living room. Pietro loves to cook for friends in this open-plan kitchen with exposed shelving. Plain white dishes and a black granite work surface continue the colour scheme.

ABOVE Three factory-style lamps hang over the long dining table in Pietro's personal apartment. On the wall, characters in four framed black-and-white photographs join in with the invited guests.
LEFT At one end of the dining room, a short black lamp provides a hat for the classical bust in this charcoal drawing. There can never be too many busts, whether two- or three-dimensional, and the ones scattered around Pescallo add a flavour of Versace, bringing opulence to these otherwise restrained interiors.

LEFT AND BELOW There's no shortage of reading material at Pescallo; nearly every room is filled with books, including second-hand or market-stall finds. Here, they do double duty as a headboard, while an Anglepoise lamp on the nightstand ensures that there'll never be any eyestrain. On shelves and tabletops, arrangements of quirky objects (below) form mini exhibitions all over the house.

OPPOSITE Pietro's style is simple and rustic. In one of the bedrooms, travelling cases – including a Chanel hatbox and a long trunk – create plenty of storage for unwanted clutter. A simple stool serves as a nightstand next to a bed covered in neutral linens.

windows from the lake. Floors at this level are of beaten cement, a material that once covered factory floors around the lake. In the kitchen area, three factory-style metal lamps hung in a row illuminate a long table that's constructed of wide planks laid horizontally, rather than lengthways. Here and there, the odd exposed stone wall contrasts with the smooth plastered walls and, together with dark wood on the upstairs floors, provides texture.

Almost all the furnishings in the house are from Pietro's business, including the sofas, tables and chairs. As for decoration, there's an eclectic combination of objects and pictures that he's gathered on his travels or picked up from markets: collections of shells, butterflies under glass, paintbrushes, smooth stones, old books, classical busts, paintings and photographs. There are vintage pieces, black-and-white contrasts, rustic wooden accents, ornate mantelpieces and quirky individual pieces.

Pietro has cleverly doubled the space in each of the rental units by creating mezzanine floors for the bedrooms. Those bedrooms may be compact, but the expansive views of the lake from their balconies extend the space and offer a sense of infinite possibility.

The chocolate and hazelnut paste *Gianduja*, or *gianduia* is famously associated with Turin. These profiteroles are stuffed with a *gianduja semifreddo*, a soft ice-cream with a base of beaten egg whites.

Profiteroles con Sorpresa

gianduja semifreddo
125 g/1 cup blanched
   toasted hazelnuts
125 g/4 oz. dark/bittersweet
   chocolate (with at least
   65 per cent cocoa solids),
   broken up
600 ml/2½ cups
   double/heavy cream
2 medium eggs, separated
175 g/1½ cups plus
   2 tablespoons icing/
   confectioners' sugar

choux pastry
75g/6 tablespoons unsalted
   butter, cubed
100 g/¾ cup plain/
   all-purpose flour, sifted
   twice with a pinch of salt
2–3 medium eggs, beaten

hot chocolate sauce, to serve

Serves 6

To make the *semifreddo*, grind the hazelnuts very finely. Put the chocolate in a heatproof bowl over a saucepan of hot water and let melt.

Put the cream in a bowl and whisk until soft peaks form, then fold in the nuts. Put the egg yolks in a second bowl with 2 tablespoons of the sugar and whisk until pale and creamy. Put the egg whites in a clean, dry bowl and whisk until soft peaks form. Add the remaining sugar to the whites, spoonful by spoonful, whisking between each addition, until very thick.

Stir the melted chocolate into the egg yolk mixture. Fold in the cream, then the meringue mixture. Spoon into a freezer container. Freeze for 12 hours until firm. Put a lined baking sheet in the freezer. Take the ice cream out of the freezer and put it in the refrigerator for 10 minutes before scooping into small balls with an ice-cream scoop and setting apart on the frozen baking sheet. Freeze until hard.

To make the choux pastry for the profiteroles, put the butter and 200 ml/1 cup water in a heavy saucepan and bring slowly to the boil, so that by the time the water boils, the butter is completely melted. As soon as it hits a rolling boil, add all the flour all at once, remove the pan from the heat and beat well with a wooden spoon. It is ready when the mixture leaves the sides of the pan.

Let cool slightly, then beat in the eggs, a little at a time, until the mixture is very smooth and shiny. If the eggs are large, it may not be necessary to add all of them. The mixture should just flop off the spoon when you bang it on the side of the pan – it should not be runny. Set teaspoons of the mixture at least 6–7 cm/3 inches apart on a lined baking sheet and bake in a preheated oven at 200°C (400°F) Gas 6 for 20–30 minutes or until deep golden brown.

Remove from the oven and split each one almost in two. Return to the oven to dry out for about 5 minutes. Cool on a wire rack. Store in a box in the freezer until needed. Pile into a dish and soften in the refrigerator for 10 minutes before serving. To assemble the profiteroles, put an ice-cream ball in each one, pushing the halves almost together, and serve with hot chocolate sauce poured over.

Il Cuore

Central Italy: Florence, Siena, Arezzo and the Maremma

2

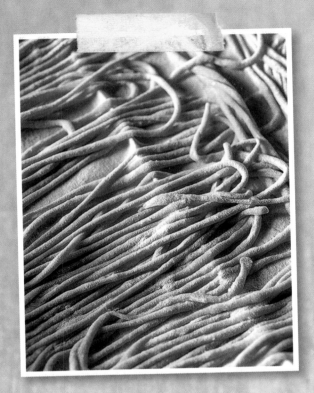

With origins in the Val d'Orcia region around Siena, *pici* is spaghetti for the greedy: a lovely, plumped-out pasta that's thick and chewy. There are few ingredients — just flour, water and, if you like, a little olive oil to make the dough easier to work with. Because it is hand-rolled, *pici* is very time-consuming to make, so it's usually reserved for special occasions. Near Montalcino, which is renowned for its *pici*, the term used is *pinci*, while in Umbria the locals call it *stringozzi*, or 'shoelaces'. The long strands are best when paired with chunky sauces such as tomato and fennel or rich porcini mushrooms.

Pici (hand-rolled pasta)

500 g/4 cups plain/
 all-purpose flour or
 Italian 00 flour, plus
 extra as necessary
1 tablespoon olive oil
sea salt
rich *ragú* or other chunky,
 hearty sauce, to serve
freshly grated Parmesan
 cheese, to serve

Serves 4–6

Sift the flour into a bowl with a good pinch of salt. Make a well in the centre and add about 150 ml/⅔ cup water and the olive oil. Mix this together with a blunt knife until it starts to come together. Try to incorporate all the flour into the dough. If it feels dry, then add a splash more water. If it feels too wet, add a sprinkling of flour. Tip out onto a floured work surface and knead for 5 minutes until smooth. Place in a plastic bag and rest the dough at room temperature for 30 minutes.

Roll the dough out to a thickness of ½ cm/¼ inch and not more than 10 cm/ 4 inches wide. Cut into ½ cm/¼ inch wide strips, 20 cm/8 inches long. Lightly oil your hands, then roll each strip of pasta on a lightly floured work surface as if it was a rolling pin until about 20.5 cm/8½ inches long. Put them on a floured tea/kitchen towel and roll the rest of the strips in the same way. Drop into a large pan of boiling salted water, stir well and bring back to the boil. Once boiling again, boil for 1 minute. Drain, reserving 1 tablespoon of the cooking water. Mix with the sauce and serve in warm bowls with plenty of freshly grated Parmesan.

love and understand the
Italians, for the people

E. M. Forster

Love and understand the Italians, for the people are more marvellous than the land.

E. M. Forster

RIGHT The entrance hall on the ground floor showcases the structural elements of this renovated farmhouse – stone steps and arches – and the building materials used to restore it: terracotta tiles and original wooden beams. A bread oven, once outside, has been incorporated into the living area of the house.
BELOW RIGHT The simple console table in the hallway was designed by the owners. Above it is a painting in the *arte povera* style showing the sacrifice of Isaac.
OPPOSITE The stone terrace at the side of the house is surrounded by tall cypresses and offers panoramic views of the Tuscan landscape.

Light and Shadow

Nearly everyone, it seems, cherishes the dream of finding an abandoned farmhouse in Tuscany and doing it up. This British couple made it happen. The interiors of their renovated farmhouse are simple, not to say monastic. And it's no wonder, for the house sits on a ridge overlooking a medieval abbey, with far-reaching views. The owners had been renting in the Chianti Classico area between Florence and Siena when they found Brogino, a rural estate with outbuildings. Once abbey property, it was just waiting for someone to bring it to life again, and fortunately, although it was empty, it wasn't wholly ruined.

LEFT AND OPPOSITE The marble-topped table was the first piece of furniture brought to the kitchen after the restoration was completed. The chairs around it have traditional woven rush seats, and the cupboards were fashioned from old walnut shutters.

BELOW A stone archway, rediscovered during the building work, leads from the hallway into the kitchen. Resting in the original bread oven is a stone water basin; both were once situated in an external courtyard.

There was a huge amount of work ahead. The ground floor would add greatly to the liveable space, but it was undeveloped at the time of purchase, and, as is traditional in rural properties, much of it was given over to the original cowsheds. Without the benefit of plumbing or an existing water supply, the enormous restoration project began. It was two years before the house was habitable. Work continued for another three years, as the couple were focused on getting the flow of the house right, with respect for the structure and the architecture. They wanted to enhance the lines of the original building, since, as they put it, 'Italian farmhouses are works of inhabitable sculpture – you should "feel" the building around you as you walk through it.'

The resulting interiors are peaceful. Walls are creamy and pale, the softness of the lime whitewash broken only by the grey outlines of stone fireplaces and doorways. A couple of bedrooms and a bathroom are painted in tones of faded yellow ochre using the raw earth pigments characteristic of the area. The owners feel that the continual play of light and shadow on walls, floors and ceilings is beautiful in itself, and needs no further enhancement.

Each of the four bedrooms is furnished with just the necessities – a bed, a chair and a wardrobe – but no clutter. 'We would rather have a few well-chosen things than a large number of objects filling up every nook and cranny,' say the owners. They took their time finding furniture, and

have acquired an eclectic mix of handmade items and locally sourced antiques. Antiques shops provided a number of pieces, including a rustic *armadio*, or wardrobe, painted with flowers, which now stands in one of the bedrooms.

Upstairs was the original *pavimento in cotto*, a flooring of terracotta tiles, while downstairs, in the area that once housed farm animals, handmade terracotta tiles were laid. The heart of the house, though, is the kitchen. Old stone door posts were used to reconstruct the fireplace, and one of the architectural triumphs of the renovation was the discovery and reincorporation of an original arched doorway. Stone steps under this arch now lead from the hallway into the kitchen, and the bread oven, which was once in an outside courtyard, was moved into the hallway.

Outdoors, more than 600 olive trees have been carefully nurtured by the owners, who wanted to celebrate the 'perennially beautiful and evocative trees' with their silvery, sage-green leaves and twisted, centuries-old trunks.

Gelato Mania

The Medici court in the Republic of Florence was famous for its frozen desserts, and it is the designer and architect Bernardo Buontalenti who is credited with having invented modern ice cream in 1565 for a Medici feast. What he created was probably a bergamot-flavoured sorbet, and there is still a street in Florence called Via delle Ghiacciaie – street of the ice-houses. Yet *gelato* has its origins in ancient Rome, Egypt and Sicily, where frozen delicacies were concocted from snow and ice brought down from the mountains and kept cold underground. The very word means 'frozen'.

In 1686, Francesco Procopio dei Coltelli, a Sicilian fisherman turned chef, devised the very first ice-cream machine, or *gelatiera*. But it wasn't until the 1920s and 1930s, when the ice-cream cart was invented, that *gelato* became popular.

The north and south of Italy have each brought different characteristics to *gelato*. In the north, the dessert is enriched with the dairy products of that region; it has a soft consistency and contains only a small amount of air. It is usually flavoured with natural ingredients such as nuts and fruit purées. In the south of the country, the lighter-textured, water-based *sorbetto* is much sweeter, with a lower fat content. *Granita* is traditionally made of shaved or scraped ice flavoured with fresh fruit or fruit or flower syrups, such as jasmine. It is popular all over Italy, but especially in Sicily, where enlightened locals enjoy it served in a brioche for breakfast.

Often sold alongside *gelato* in ice-cream parlours is the mousse-like *semifreddo*, a 'partly cold' type of *gelato* mixed in equal parts with whipped cream. By law, Italian *gelato* must contain at least 3.5% butterfat; there is no upper limit!

This hearty Tuscan soup is always better the day after you make it, and indeed the word *ribollita* means 'boiled again'. It can be, and often is, made with odds and ends, but it always contains cannellini beans, potato, leftover bread, *cavolo nero* (you can substitute kale or Savoy cabbage), olive oil and herbs. Unlike its closest relative, *minestrone*, the soup does not contain any pasta. Instead, in most versions, chunks of bread are stirred in with the vegetables and broth. Here, the soup is ladled over thick slices of toasted bread rubbed with garlic, and generously sprinkled with Parmesan.

La Ribollita

250 g/1½ cups dried cannellini beans
150 ml/⅔ cup extra virgin olive oil, plus extra to drizzle
1 onion, finely chopped
1 carrot, chopped
1 celery stalk, chopped
2 leeks, finely chopped
4 garlic cloves, finely chopped, plus 1 extra peeled and bruised for rubbing
1 small white (Dutch) cabbage, shredded
1 large potato, peeled and chopped
4 medium courgettes/zucchini, chopped
400 ml/1¾ cups Italian sieved tomato *passata*
2 sprigs fresh rosemary
2 sprigs fresh thyme
2 sprigs fresh sage
1 whole dried red chilli/chile
500 g/1 lb *cavolo nero* (Tuscan black winter cabbage) or Savoy cabbage, finely sliced
sea salt and freshly ground black pepper
6 thick slices coarse crusty white bread
freshly grated Parmesan cheese, to serve

Soak the cannellini beans overnight in plenty of cold water.

Heat half the olive oil in a heavy stockpot and add the onion, carrot and celery. Cook gently for about 10 minutes, stirring frequently. Next add the leeks and finely chopped garlic and cook for another 10 minutes. Add the white cabbage, potato and courgettes/zucchini, stir well and cook for 10 minutes, stirring frequently.

Stir in the drained soaked beans, *passata*, herb sprigs, dried chilli/chile, salt and plenty of black pepper. Cover with about 2 litres/quarts water (the vegetables should be well covered) and bring to the boil, then turn down the heat and simmer, covered, for at least 2 hours until the beans are very soft.

Transfer 2–3 large ladlefuls of soup to a bowl and mash well using the back of the ladle. Return to the soup to thicken it. Stir in the *cavolo nero* and simmer for another 15 minutes. Allow to cool, then refrigerate overnight.

The next day, slowly reheat the soup and stir in the remaining olive oil. Toast the bread and rub with the bruised garlic clove. Arrange the bread over the base of a tureen or individual bowls and ladle the soup over it. Drizzle with extra olive oil and serve with plenty of freshly grated Parmesan.

Serves 8

ABOVE AND RIGHT Under a loggia stretching the length of the house, a cluster of benches and chairs sport fabrics designed by Isabelle de Borchgrave (above). In the hallway (right), once a cow byre, her decorative painted stripes echo the pure lines of Jean Philippe Gauvin's stairway. The floral motif on the open cupboard is also Isabelle's work.

La Querciola

When Werner and Isabelle de Borchgrave first found La Querciola, it was hard to see beyond the rubble. The Tuscan farmhouse, part of a country estate of abandoned buildings, was in a parlous condition, its ceiling having caved in, filling the building with shards of *tegole*, the traditional roofing tiles. With stalls for livestock on the ground floor and living quarters on the first floor, this house was typical of the region; at one point, some 30 peasants had inhabited the first floor.

LEFT The proportions of the hallway are grand enough to accommodate this large lantern fitted with green-tinted glass. A shadowy grey colour highlights architectural features such as arches, and stands out against the soft warm yellow of the walls.
BELOW Downstairs, a kitchen has been carved from a series of rooms that once housed farm animals.
OPPOSITE Warm, earthy colours – like those of terracotta itself – are the background for the medieval motifs Isabelle painted on the walls of her sitting room. Rich tones are also characteristic of her textiles, which here cover plump cushions.

Along with three other families, the de Borchgraves bought La Querciola, planning to divide the cost of renovation between them and then to use the farmhouse as a shared summer home. Before renovation started, they enlisted the help of French architect Jean Philippe Gauvin. Purity, simplicity and clean lines are the hallmarks of Jean Philippe's architectural style, and it was exactly these qualities that the de Borchgraves wanted him to bring to the restoration of the derelict farmhouse. In common with Werner and Isabelle, Jean Philippe was anxious to respect the original lines of La Querciola and to retain its atmosphere, for, as Werner notes, 'This type of house imposes on you what it already is. The proportions are so nice that you don't want to change them.'

They agreed on a policy of minimum intervention, but their first challenge was deciding upon where exactly to site the staircase, since the original staircase was located outside, in keeping with traditional regional style. Jean Philippe's solution was a simple, narrow staircase that rises through the centre of the house. The new skylight inserted above it transformed what was previously a dark and unloved space into a vibrant and active core of the house.

Downstairs, the generous proportions of the original vaulted cow byres offered an opportunity to create more liveable space, and yet the ground floor was very dark. Jean Philippe effectively transformed this area by installing large glass doors at either end of the space, allowing light to pour in from the outside; white-painted walls further brighten

the rooms. A simple refectory table is the perfect foil for the contemporary kitchen appliances that hug the wall of one of the former cow stalls. A bright corridor leads out onto a loggia running the length of the red-brick house. On a hot day, a vine-covered pergola provides shade, while a vast blue sky hangs over the rectangular swimming pool.

Upstairs, where the peasant farmers once lived and slept in five rooms on the first floor, huddling round a vast central fireplace, the space has been extended up into the attic to create nine new bedrooms, each one with its own bathroom. The palette changes here from the airy lightness of the ground floor to a rich glow; colours are earthy and warm, with touches of medieval-style decoration provided by Isabelle, who is a talented artist. Isabelle drew much inspiration from the design and colour of the Piero della Francesca frescoes in the Basilica of San Francesco in nearby

Arezzo, even climbing the scaffolding when they were being restored so that she could inspect them close up, 'nose to wall', as her husband says.

The grand spaces of La Querciola cried out for large and imposing pieces of furniture, and Arezzo's monthly antiques market came to the rescue. Other pieces were sourced from Indonesia. Their simple yet majestic lines are softened by plump cushions and by Isabelle's hand-painted textiles.

OPPOSITE The pink blush of a huge painted wooden cupboard contrasts with the bare, scrubbed wood dining table and brings inside a warm colour more typically used outside.
ABOVE In the upstairs living room, a massive fireplace takes centre stage. A deep armchair is upholstered in emerald-green linen and set against a patterned rug. A palette of wheat and rich ochre is carefully graduated along the walls of a room that would originally have been occupied by several families.

LEFT Wooden armchairs with straw seating make this upstairs loggia a haven of relaxation, where afternoon sunlight filters through gauzy curtains that are the same shade as the walls.

OPPOSITE AND BELOW Before the comforts of central heating, people often kept their rooms warm by hanging tapestries and other textiles on the walls; this practice also prevented damp. Isabelle's painted curtain is in keeping with the medieval-style work in the rest of the house, decorated with small clusters of circles that match its plaited border. Pale and delicate as it is, the curtain stands out in a room where the beams and furniture are similarly understated.

Dining Al Fresco

In E. M. Forster's *A Room with a View*, the heroine Lucy Honeychurch is suddenly and passionately kissed when she wanders off from a picnic in the hills above Florence. Not all picnics are as dramatic, but there is surely something about eating outside that encourages feelings of warmth and conviviality. When dining *al fresco*, Italians usually take the opportunity to gather together as many family members and friends as possible.

Thanks to the Mediterranean climate, Italy enjoys a gentle spring and a long summer, and during these months people eat outdoors whenever they can. The area immediately surrounding a country villa or a city apartment is considered an extension of that property's inside space. Many country houses boast a pergola

humming with bees and birdlife, and meals are spread out under its shade, for the summer sun can be fierce. A vast umbrella is likely to protect the terrace of a city apartment, and a panoramic view only enhances the drink taken at the end of the day.

The *sagra*, a special feast or festival dedicated to one type of food, is a quintessential part of an Italian summer. For weeks beforehand, colourful roadside posters announce the date of the event. Then, on the evening in question, not only families but entire villages gather together at long tables placed end to end, while the women of the town prepare and serve the featured dish. Music and dancing follow, all lit by the glow of citronella candles, whose sharp, citrus scent repels uninvited guests: mosquitoes. Popular Umbrian *sagre* are the *Sagra della cipolla* (onion) in Cannara, the *Sagra del Buon Mangiare* (eating well) in San Faustino and the *Sagra della Macedonia* (fruit salad) in Marsciano.

OPPOSITE One of a series of rooms connected by a doorless enfilade, the dining area is part of the new extension. The table base was designed by Mark Brazier-Jones.

LEFT The sleek kitchen is the perfect place for Anna's husband, a food industry professional, to experiment, using produce from the adjacent *orto* (garden). The sink is made from a block of basalt.

BELOW This 1950s Maremma farmhouse looks like it's been there for ever, yet the guiding aesthetic when renovating it was the idea of transitory beauty. In the same way that leather, terracotta and iron improve with age, all the imperfections it embodies have only added to its fascination.

Buddhist Baroque

You might expect the owner of Contemporanea, a stylish furniture, art and lighting gallery with branches in Rome and London, to live in a gently decaying *palazzo* – either that, or perhaps a picturesque, sprawling farmhouse located in carefully cultivated countryside. But instead, Anna Garcea has boldly taken the best of modern, 20th-century Italian architecture and married it to her own taste for what she describes as 'minimalist baroque', a style that is also celebrated at Contemporanea.

Around Capalbio, the nearest town, it's possible to lose yourself somewhere between the expansive plains, the groves of pines and cypresses, the clumps of rosemary and the sandy coastline. It's one of the few remaining wild places in this part of southern Tuscany, and in what was once social housing for farm workers clearing malarial swamps in the Maremma, Anna has fashioned a country residence in which extravagant touches contrast with the spare lines of a 1950s building.

LEFT Next to a head cast by Oliviero Rinaldi is an empty frame by the Japanese designer Mineko. Both stand on a cabinet made of plastered wood, with doors by Gennaro Avallone in plaster over canvas. The white cushions and leather bench are from Contemporanea.
BELOW Space for a small study area, with tables designed by Mark Brazier-Jones, has been found on this landing; the black bookcase is made of stained chestnut. The lamp alone adds a Rococo touch.
OPPOSITE Tucked under the travertine staircase is the single antique in the house: an 18th-century painted French cabinet. The huge plaster fireplace is from Contemporanea.

Structurally, the house has been left much as Anna found it, apart from the addition of a small wing to incorporate a dining area and more living space. She wanted to retain the spirit of the place without detracting from its humble origins, so the new wing was crafted from iron and glass to a modernist design in black. What you see from a distance is not the new wing but the masonry and original proportions of the existing rural structure. It stands square and stolid, as rooted in the landscape as the vineyards around it.

One of the most striking features of the ground-floor interiors is the doorless enfilade that threads through the rooms downstairs, connecting them like railway carriages. At the heart of it all is the kitchen. Its door opens onto the adjacent *orto*, the kitchen garden, allowing for delectable seasonal meals. The absence of doors contributes to a wonderful sense of space and is in keeping with the minimalist side of the owner's style. There are no bulging walls here, no rounded corners. The one exception is the grand fireplace in the sitting room, its chimney breast swelling gently outwards like a Baroque scroll. Everything else is squared off, at right angles, including the staircase, made of travertine. It's a work of uncompromising beauty.

RIGHT Old lace cushions and wooden panelling recall the 18th century in the master bedroom, which is painted a soft grey. To prevent a full-scale slip into the past, Anna has placed a modern lamp by British designer Mark Brazier-Jones on the bedside table; his work is sold in Contemporanea.

Upstairs are three bedrooms with ensuites, a reading nook and an office. The main bedroom would not be out of place in an elegant Parisian flat rather than this example of modest social housing in the Maremma. The original walls have been lined with 18th-century-style wooden panelling accentuated with classical details. The room itself is tiny, with a bathroom that is simultaneously plain and opulent: high ceilings, bare floorboards and a massive Philippe Starck bathtub, whose puritanical hardware makes an exciting contrast to the crystal chandelier hanging above it.

Anna has opted for a Buddhist aesthetic of ephemeral beauty, but, paradoxically, using materials that will stand the test of time. It's a difficult recipe to perfect, but its success can be judged by the peace and serenity of the house. Her friends haven't stopped asking her for the secret.

LEFT Anna's style of opposites is captured perfectly in this bathroom, where modern taps/faucets crown a traditional, hand-cut stone basin. Above it, an elaborate mirror balances the minimalist aesthetic with ornate fripperies at its corners.
OPPOSITE The elegant crystal chandelier dangling over this deep modern bathtub by Philippe Starck appears to have wandered out of the dining room and found its way into the bathroom. To achieve the effect on the walls, colour was added to a water base and the mixture applied to wet plaster. Bleached floorboards and bare walls complete the look in a very atypical ensuite.

I Giardini

The early Italian garden reached perfection during the Renaissance. Before then, gardens were secret places enclosed by high walls, which functioned as quiet spots for contemplation and prayer or were devoted to growing medicinal herbs or fruits.

The Renaissance garden, too, offered a retreat from the world. Some of the most famous Italian gardens were created by cardinals fleeing from intrigues at the papal court. Many rulers saw them as a status symbol to demonstrate their power and magnificence. Yet just as often, the vast, open spaces provided a place to frolic, to play philosophical games or even tricks. At Bomarzo, in Lazio, giant animals, strange monsters and tilted buildings tip the visitor into the realms of fantasy in the garden commissioned by Pier Francesco Orsini.

Water refreshes the weary during the heat of an Italian summer. At the Villa d'Este at Tivoli, it cascades down sculpted terraces and spurts up in feathery columns, while at the Villa Lante at Bagnaia grottoes drip with moisture and capricious jets, or *giochi d'acqua*, tease the unsuspecting visitor. The fabulous gardens at Isola Bella on Lake Maggiore seem to hover, magical and dreamlike, at the water's edge.

The tropical garden of composer William Walton, La Mortella ('the myrtle'), is found on the island of Ischia, and a short boat ride to Capri will take you to the lush gardens of Axel Munthe's Villa San Michele. Between Rome and Naples lie the romantic gardens of Ninfa, a place where roses clamber over the remains of an ancient city, and luxuriant vegetation is reflected in a stream meandering through the ruins.

The gardens at Isola Bella on Lake Maggiore seem to hover, magical and dreamlike, at the water's edge.

Panzanella is one of those concoctions that turn out to be much more delicious than its constituent ingredients might promise. The key thing is that everything should be as fresh as possible – except for the bread, which must be completely stale or, failing that, toasted to make it as dry as possible. Water is then added to soften it and break it into small chunks or crumbs depending on taste or the recipe.

Panzanella is popular in both Tuscany and Umbria, where *cucina povera* or 'poor man's cuisine' means making do with what's to hand. There are as many variations to it as there are towns where it is eaten, but the staples are bread, tomatoes, olive oil, onions and salt. Basil, olives, capers and cucumbers make tasty additions, although with this salad the general rule of 'less is more' is a good one to follow.

Panzanella

1 red onion, finely chopped
200 g/7 oz. crusty Italian
    white bread
3 tablespoons red wine
    vinegar
500 g/1 lb. ripe tomatoes
4 tablespoons extra virgin
    olive oil
1 garlic clove, crushed
a handful fresh basil leaves,
    torn
sea salt and freshly
    ground black pepper

Serves 4

Place the onion in a bowl, add 1 teaspoon of salt and cover with cold water. Set aside for 1 hour, then drain well and pat dry.

About 15 minutes before making the salad, cut or tear the bread into bite-sized chunks and place in a large bowl. Add the vinegar, stir well and set aside. Cut the tomatoes into chunks about the same size as the bread and place to drain in a sieve over a bowl.

When ready to serve, press the tomatoes a little to extract any remaining juices and place in the bowl with the bread. Add the drained onion.

Whisk the olive oil, tomato juices, garlic and some salt and pepper together and stir into the salad until really well combined. Transfer to a serving bowl and scatter over the basil. Serve at once.

Italian Cheeses

The art of cheese-making was perfected in the *caseale*, the Ancient Romans' cheese kitchen. The Romans were the first to smoke cheese, and their skills spread across Europe along with their empire. Today, Italy is famed for its *gorgonzola*, *parmigiano* and *mozzarella*, made from cow's or buffalo's milk. But there are more than 450 other ancient and humble cheeses that deserve to be better known.

Cousin to the blue-veined *gorgonzola* is the milder, creamier *dolcelatte*, or 'sweet milk'. *Burrata* is a *mozzarella* with a creamy liquid centre and, like *dolcelatte*, it is much softer than its relative.

Italy is famed for its gorgonzola, parmigiano and mozzarella. But there are more than 450 other cheeses that deserve to be better known.

The making of sharp, piquant *asiago d'Allevo* cheese dates back a thousand years or more. A hard cheese of unpasteurized cow's milk, it is native to the Veneto, and is suitable for grating and for use in cooking. Another cow's milk cheese from the north, *taleggio* has been around since the tenth century. Fairly soft, it has a thin, creased rind, and develops earthy tones with age. The hard cheese *pecorino toscano*, as its name indicates, is made from the milk of sheep (*pecore*) raised in the Maremma in Tuscany, where it has been produced for over 2,500 years. A young *pecorino* is mild; ageing brings out a sharper, nuttier taste. This cheese is often flavoured with wine or herbs, or preserved in ash. Sicilian *pecorino* was mentioned in Homer's *Odyssey*.

Ricotta, or 'recooked' cheese, is soft in texture and mild in flavour, qualities that make it popular for sweet and savoury dishes alike. *Mascarpone*, on the other hand, is a thick, creamy liquid cheese that's used almost exclusively for the popular dessert *tiramisù*.

Theatrical Designs

It's the cardinal rule with any major purchase: think long and hard about it and, whatever you do, don't buy on a whim. But that's exactly what this couple did. Within hours of seeing this stone farmhouse for the first time, they had made up their minds. A long, low stone building outside of Siena, Le Porciglia — 'the pigsties' — was built in the 19th century and had been empty for many years. The house was larger than most and, unusually, it had its own chapel.

ABOVE LEFT In a protected area of the garden, weathered and sun-bleached tables play host to two terracotta sculptures.
ABOVE RIGHT Patterned, handmade Sicilian tiles brighten the kitchen work surfaces. A 19th-century Tuscan plate rack hangs over a large stone sink that was custom made.

RIGHT Wire birdcage lanterns rest atop a plain table made by designer Piet Hein Eek; the gently curved white chairs are Indonesian. Under vaulting that recalls the interior of a church, arches lead from the dining room to the working area of the kitchen. The floor is laid with antique flagstones from Lecce.

OPPOSITE AND FAR LEFT The drama of this magnificent living room is heightened by the wooden balustrading from a theatre that burned down in the 1920s. The Dutch chairs and the fireplace are both 17th century. The table just seen to the right of the archway is covered with an Indian cloth. A primitive model of the Archangel Gabriel (far left) presides here, along with two lamps fashioned from candlesticks. Between them hangs a bright red ceremonial African headdress; to their left, a stack of boules and a piece of fencing armour.
LEFT The galleried corridor is paved with terracotta tiles set in beige cement.

Simone de Looze is an interior decorator who also deals in antiques, as her mother did before her. So it is not surprising that she was ready to get stuck into a project for which she already had definite ideas. 'When I was still a little girl, I started to collect clippings from interiors magazines, and over all the years my taste for the things I'd like in a southern European country house has not changed.'

The first move for Simone was to contact the English designer Anthony Collett of Collett-Zarzycki. With a house of his own in Tuscany, he was aware of the challenges, and his cool, clean approach to architecture and design harmonized with their own. They also took on an Italian architect, Carlos von Rex. His help was invaluable when it came to obtaining the permits needed before a historic house can be altered, and his facility with three languages smoothed the way. Together, he and Collett devised a plan that would make sense of the huge, 'rather ungainly' space. Besides the chapel, the property had stables, pigsties and barns, and the aim was a house that was comfortable and friendly, while allowing everyone their privacy.

With its double-height ceiling, the living room is the set piece of the house. While the owners could have eked out two more bedrooms upstairs, their idea was to open up this area instead. The light, airy space they created stretches right up to the old beams, and a corridor leading to four of the main bedrooms now projects into the dramatic heart of this house. It is supported by carved wooden beams and edged by a balustraded gallery salvaged from a 20th-century theatre destroyed by fire. The master bedroom boasts an iron balcony, and it, too, faces the living room below. Two magnificent 19th-century chandeliers from a hotel in the south of France dangle from the ceiling overhead, and the effect of the whole is surprising and unexpected.

One of the most intriguing architectural elements is to be found underfoot. 'It was a dream to experiment with the floors in Le Porciglia…the variations were endless.' Nearly all of the floors have different patterns, and the one along the bedroom corridor is particularly interesting. Since that floor had to be created anew, Simone's solution was to set old and new terracotta tiles – upside down – in beige cement squares to form a chequerboard pattern. The delightfully undulating surface of the original floors has been left in many of the rooms, while the flooring in another bedroom features an octagonal brick pattern. And if a bedroom was lost in opening up their living space, no matter: there is a guest cottage in a barn next to the pool.

The calm exuded by this house must have something to do with its cool tones. Colour is only an accent, never the main attraction. Your eye might not drop to the *zoccolo*, a grey stripe at floor level, but you'll surely notice the 20th-century Sicilian tiles lining the alcoves in the bathroom and kitchen walls. Simone felt strongly about this neutral palette.

'I don't like the use of much colour in rustic houses. The objects and furniture all have a story to tell, and they do that better against a neutral background.' It's against that very background that Simone was able to set her many antique pieces, some of them Italian, others Dutch and French. 'One learns that decorating is all about the right objects put together in the right way.'

Of course, none of this wizardry was accomplished quickly. It took, Simone says, all of five years. But it was important to get things right, and the time the family took to restore Le Porciglia was an appropriate counterbalance to the speed at which they bought their dream.

LEFT AND BELOW The marble bathtub, from the mid-17th century, comes from Livorno, as does the tin mirror. In the galleried corridor (inset below), Puglian pots stand sentry on a 17th-century cupboard.
OPPOSITE For this Tuscan bedroom, it seems fitting that cypress trees should be the motif on an Indian textile that hangs in the place of a headboard. Two delightfully irregular mirrors hang over half-moon console tables that double as nightstands. The bedcover is white, with a pattern of fruit and flowers.

THIS PAGE Le Porciglia is a sprawling farmhouse with its own chapel. The beautiful stonework, tiled roof and arched doorways seen here are all typical of Tuscan architecture.

Many legends surround these soft, pillowy biscuits: it is said that they were shaped to resemble the Madonna's eyes in Renaissance paintings, and also that the recipe was brought back from the Crusades. The truth is that their delicate flavour and sweetness are the perfect foil for a strong coffee. Grind the almonds yourself for a fresher flavour.

Ricciarelli

175 g/1¼ cups whole blanched almonds, finely ground, or 175 g/1¾ cups ground almonds

200 g/1 cup caster/superfine sugar, plus extra for rolling

½ teaspoon baking powder

1 tablespoon plain/all-purpose flour

1 large egg white

2–3 drops bitter almond extract

icing/confectioners' sugar, sifted, to serve

Makes
16–20 Biscuits

Preheat the oven to 200°C (400°F) Gas 6.

Put the ground almonds in a bowl with the caster/superfine sugar. Sift the baking powder with the flour into the almonds and sugar. In a separate, grease-free bowl, whisk the egg white until stiff but not dry, then stir into the almond mixture. Add the almond extract and blend until you have a soft malleable paste.

Pour some caster/superfine sugar onto a plate. Roll the paste into long sausages, then cut into fingers. Roll each one in the sugar, then press into the traditional oval or diamond shape by tapering the ends and flattening slightly with your palm.

Arrange the *ricciarelli* on a baking sheet (preferably lined with baking parchment to prevent over-browning). Bake in the preheated oven for 10–12 minutes until pale golden. They will puff up and spread a little. Do not overbake or they will be too hard. Transfer to a wire rack to cool. Press the tops into icing/confectioners' sugar or simply roll in icing/confectioners' sugar and pile high on a plate.

Il Sud 3

Rome, the Amalfi Coast and Apulia

ladri di biciclette
di Vittorio de Sica

Joseph E. Levine
presents

Boccaccio '70

produced by
Carlo Ponti

An Embassy Pictures Release
Distributed by 20th Century-Fox

Music by
Nino Rota and
Armando Trovajoli

in EASTMAN COLOUR

SOPHIA LOREN   **ROMY SCHNEIDER**   **ANITA EKBERG**

DE SICA   VISCONTI   FELLINI

Cinema Paradiso

Who can forget Federico Fellini's voluptuous shot of Anita Ekberg splashing in Rome's Trevi Fountain in *La Dolce Vita*, or Michelangelo Antonioni's existential masterpiece *L'Avventura*? Italian cinema has won more Academy Awards for Best Foreign Language Film than any other country.

Cinecittà, the vast studio complex outside Rome, was founded in 1937 by Mussolini, and most of its early films were fascist propaganda. The end of the Second World War, however, ushered in the golden age of Italian cinema, with Neorealist classics such as Roberto Rossellini's *Rome, Open City* (1945), Vittorio de Sica's *The Bicycle Thieves* (1948) and Luchino Visconti's *La Terra Trema* (1948), which was based on Giovanni Verga's acclaimed novel about a family of Sicilian fishermen.

The much lighter comedies of the 1950s reflected the country's changing fortunes and were the perfect vehicle for stars such as Claudia Cardinale, Vittorio Gassman, Gina Lollobrigida, Marcello Mastroianni and Sophia Loren. Those years also saw the rise of the Neapolitan actor Totò, a mimic whose facial gestures contributed to the phenomenal popularity of the satires he starred in.

In the 1960s, serious political films such as Gillo Pontecorvo's *The Battle of Algiers* (1966) were counterbalanced by the low-budget but exceptionally successful Spaghetti Westerns. Meanwhile, Visconti re-emerged with *The Leopard* and *Rocco and His Brothers*, followed by *Death in Venice* in 1971.

Giuseppe Tornatore's poignant *Cinema Paradiso* (1988) was an homage to the magic of film. It celebrated the enduring romance of cinema, and the widespread Italian custom of showing movies outdoors under the stars during the warm summer months.

Caprese means 'from Capri', an island just off the tip of the Sorrento peninsula in the Campania region around Naples. This salad, dressed in the colours of the Italian flag – green, white and red – is a favourite on menus around the world, along with the cake that shares its name (see pages 148–149). The finest buffalo mozzarella also comes from Campania, so in common with many Italian dishes, the salad is a happy marriage of the best of local produce. Ideally, it should be made with almost overripe tomatoes.

Insalata Caprese

450 g/1 lb. buffalo
   mozzarella, sliced or torn
   (if you can get your hands
   on it, *Caseificio Corvino
   Mozzarella di Bufala
   Campana* is unparalleled)
about 8 ripe Italian plum
   tomatoes, e.g. Martino,
   Perini, San Marzano,
   sliced
a large handful fresh basil
   leaves
finest quality extra virgin
   olive oil, to drizzle
freshly ground sea salt and
   black pepper
a handful rocket/arugula
   leaves, to serve (optional)
good-quality Italian bread,
   to serve

Serves 4

Serve this salad however it suits you. Simply lay a line of tomato slices next to a line of mozzarella slices on a serving platter. Season, then either tear the basil leaves or leave whole and scatter all over.

Instead, stick to the old-fashioned way and lay the tomato and mozzarella slices alternately on the platter, season and scatter the whole or torn basil leaves as above. Add a handful of rocket/arugula leaves, if using. Generously drizzle the olive oil over the salad and serve.

You could also simply divide the ingredients as above between 4 plates and then finish off the salad with the olive oil. Serve with any good-quality Italian bread.

The Merchants' Palace

It pays to have good friends. A few years ago, Marco Livadiotti was tipped off by one of his about a derelict house for sale on the Amalfi Coast. There, at the crossroads of past cultures – Spanish, Turkish, Arabic – Livadiotti discovered a treasure clinging to the cliffs above the sea, surrounded by fragrant lemon trees.

LEFT This former 18th-century merchants' house on the Amalfi Coast is tinted in the faded colours of the sunset, or perhaps the fruit growing on the hill behind it – *fico d'India*, or prickly pear.
ABOVE From one of several balconies, the owner can look towards Raito, the nearest village, or out over the Gulf of Salerno.

LEFT Vines climb the surrounding hills in centuries-old terraces. On this side of the property, door frames are outlined in green. **BELOW LEFT** Shadows thrown from the railings of a balcony echo the exotic patterns on the owner's textiles and pottery. Many of the church towers on the Amalfi Coast are covered in *maiolica* tiles.

ABOVE Lemons are the chief ingredient of *limoncello*. To be authentic, it must come from the Amalfi Coast. **OPPOSITE** A clutch of goblets, a manual typewriter, a candelabra and a bowl of fruit — the owner loves rearranging the props in these frescoed rooms. The *maiolica* floor tiles were made locally.

For a man who has lived most of his life in Yemen, the house seemed the perfect fit. It was built in 1760 for Amalfi merchants who traded in textiles with the Orient, and now it is decorated with Yemeni and Iranian carpets and textiles. Even the ceramic tiles underfoot have a sort of Eastern exoticism, though they are locally made.

Everyone who visits the palazzo comments on its positive energy, which seems strange given the disastrous condition it was in when Marco bought it. Yet all the years of abandonment had done nothing to destroy its incredible fascination, perhaps because the place had never undergone any major changes. The fact that the house had remained nearly intact was of great importance to Marco, who has nourished a lifelong passion for architecture and the way it interacts with its environment.

So Marco began the mammoth work of restoration, including the installation of a sewer system, electricity and bathrooms. The work seemed unending. Doors, windows and flooring had to be rebuilt, even ceilings — all of which were frescoed and needed careful preservation. Over two levels and 650 square metres/7000 square feet, Marco used traditional materials including terracotta, wood, stone, whitewash and plaster. In

RIGHT This grouping of bright jugs and mugs is a beautiful still life atop a marble ledge. **BELOW AND OPPOSITE BELOW** Below is the *palazzo's* summer kitchen; below opposite its winter kitchen. Both have bread ovens dating from the 1700s; a selection of tiles is spread over the top of the winter one. An array of woven baskets decorate the hearth in the summer kitchen, which is still being restored.

places, he resorted to cement bricks mixed with lime for, as he says, one can't always be traditional: times change and it's important to know how best to adapt modern materials and to understand where to use them. Marco greatly enjoyed recreating the house's internal landscape, the paths through it, the layout and the flow. In every house, he says, you must create your own route – opening and closing doors until you find it.

The house is entered through an arcade dating from 1800. A vast hall on the ground floor leads into an old 19th-century 'winter kitchen' with ceramic tiles and cellars below it. Underneath the cellars are three wells, all still working. There is also another 'summer kitchen', which looks out onto the garden and from there over the Gulf of Salerno. Both kitchens have bread ovens from the 1700s. The summer kitchen is rustic and very old, and Marco is still in the process of restoring it. Sometimes he and his friends from all over the world eat there. Everyone cooks together, sharing the flavours of France, Germany and the Middle East, and wherever they eat the view is splendid, whether it's of the coast or the village of Raito. At night, they eat by candlelight under the stars, listening to the ships coming and going from the port of Salerno.

From the summer kitchen, there are stairs to the *piano nobile*, and a succession of vaulted, frescoed rooms, one after the other. The eight rooms are laid with traditional terracotta floors from the late 1700s or ornamented with tiles from a century later. Four of the rooms are bedrooms, and there is also a dining hall, two living rooms and a studio. Each looks over garden, sea or towards the mountains, while air from the sea and the mountains creates counter currents as it flows through the interiors. Visiting friends prefer to stay inside, insisting that this magical house is like a village in which it's possible to explore every corner.

OPPOSITE A wonderfully varied aesthetic informs the furniture and decoration throughout the house. Instead of stuffing its rooms, with their vast proportions and high, vaulted ceilings, with large, bulky pieces, the owner has opted to let the architecture and the frescoes speak for themselves. Here, mid-century wooden furniture and a curvaceous metal and leather rocker create a small study area in a corner of one of the living rooms.

THIS PAGE AND OPPOSITE An Eastern flavour pervades this house, whose first owners traded textiles with the East; Marco Livadiotti has spent much of his life in Yemen. In the two bedrooms shown here, his own textiles dress both chairs and floors, challenging, perhaps, the ceramic tiles in the room beyond (above). Most of the internal doors had to be remade; the terrace doors are picked out in bright green. Furniture is simple and understated — the wooden frames of these leather chairs can be folded up and the chairs moved to another room. A large cut-out of a bull keeps things from getting too serious (left).

Inside, there's little furniture or decoration. Frescoes provide the drama, and Marco is constantly moving things around, giving some away, bringing in others to take their place on 'a stage on which even the objects have life and a role to play'. Nothing is there by chance, for 'a house is an extension of yourself'.

Marco, who now restores houses for a living, wanted to save one of the few remaining original 18th-century *palazzi* along the coast and return it to its original splendour. He's managed it in part, though it's a work in progress. He hopes to finish one day, but it may take him 20 years or more. When he finishes, he'll go, he says. Maybe. But here, where the light constantly changes, the colours change with it, making the house take on a new character every few hours. Perhaps he'll never leave…

120

Maiolica and Italian Ceramics

It's rare to find an Italian town that doesn't have at least one shop selling local ceramics. They are a traditional feature of Italian life, and make a beautiful gift to take home from a holiday.

Maiolica, or tin-glazed earthenware, dates all the way back to the Renaissance, when brightly coloured scenes from history, legend or sometimes even Biblical subjects began to appear on ceramics. Classical and religious subjects could be gruesome, whereas mythological ones were often playfully suggestive. Production was concentrated in central Italy, and special colours or colour combinations came to be associated with different manufacturing cities such as Gubbio and Deruta, Urbino and Faenza. *Maiolica* from Gubbio, in northern Umbria, is still typically garnet red, pink or greenish-yellow, whereas blue and orange are more common on the pottery from Urbino, a town further east in the Marche. In Orvieto, at the border of Tuscany, Umbria and Lazio, some *maiolica* is still based on medieval Islamic designs featuring birds or mermaids, and is coloured green and white, while grotesque decoration regularly features on *maiolica* from Deruta, in Umbria.

Maiolica comes in a vast range of traditional shapes, including cups, bowls, plates, trays and different sizes of elegant containers. Two-handled jugs, whether rounded or flat, are mostly reserved for decoration, while the more common single-handled jugs are still used at table. Tall, narrow apothecary jars are often filled with fresh or dried flower arrangements

Nowadays, *maiolica* is much used for display, but it is also possible to order impressive dinner sets from major manufacturing centres such as Deruta.

SALITA
DE BARBIERI

30.

When visiting the city of Naples in 1889, King Umberto I and Queen Margherita of Savoy summoned the city's most famous *pizzaiolo* (pizza maker), Raffaele Esposito, and asked to taste the local delicacy. Raffaele presented the royal couple with three choices: a pizza with lard, cheese and basil; one with garlic, oil and tomatoes; and another with tomato, mozzarella and basil – the colours of the Italian flag. Suitably patriotic, the Queen chose the last as her favourite, and to honour her, it was given her name. Whether this legend can be believed or not, it's certain that this pizza is a favourite the world over.

Pizza Margherita

½ recipe Basic Pizza Dough (see below)
50–75 g/2–3 oz. buffalo mozzarella or cow's milk mozzarella (*fior di latte*)
3–4 tablespoons good-quality fresh tomato sauce
200 g/7 oz. very ripe cherry tomatoes, halved
a handful fresh basil leaves
extra virgin olive oil, to drizzle
sea salt and freshly ground black pepper

basic pizza dough
25 g/1 cake compressed fresh yeast, 1 tablespoon/ packet active dry yeast or 2 teaspoons fast-action dried/ quick-rising yeast
½ teaspoon sugar
250 ml/1 cup hand-hot water
500 g/4 cups unbleached white bread flour or Italian 0 or 00 flour, plus extra as necessary
1 teaspoon fine sea salt
1 tablespoon olive oil, plus extra for oiling

*Makes 1
25 cm/10 inch
pizza*

First make the dough. In a medium bowl, cream the fresh yeast with the sugar and beat in the water. Leave for 10 minutes until frothy. For other yeasts, follow the manufacturers' instructions. Sift the flour and salt into a large bowl and make a well in the centre. Pour in the yeast mixture, then the olive oil. Mix together with a round-bladed knife, then using hands until the dough comes together. Tip out onto a lightly floured work surface, then with clean dry hands knead briskly for 5–10 minutes until smooth, shiny and elastic. If it is too soft to handle, knead in a little more flour. Shape into a ball, put in a clean oiled bowl, cover with a damp tea/kitchen towel and let rise for about 1½ hours until doubled in size.

Put a large, heavy baking sheet on the lower shelf of the oven, Preheat the oven to 220°C (425°F) Gas 7 for at least 30 minutes.

Lightly squeeze excess moisture out of the mozzarella, and roughly slice it.

Uncover the dough, punch out the air and roll into a 25-cm/10-inch circle directly onto non-stick baking parchment. Slide this onto a pizza peel or rimless baking sheet. Spread the tomato sauce over the pizza base, leaving a 1-cm/½-inch rim around the edge. Scatter with the tomatoes and season. Open the oven door and slide paper and pizza onto the hot baking sheet.

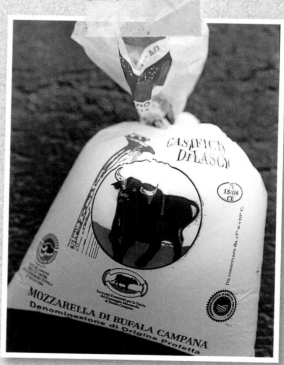

Bake for 5 minutes, remove from the oven and scatter the mozzarella over the tomatoes. Return the pizza to the oven without the paper. Bake for a further 15 minutes or until the crust is golden and the cheese melted but still white. Remove from the oven, scatter with the basil leaves and drizzle with olive oil. Eat immediately.

LEFT A black lacquer tray from Thailand keeps company with a bronze Neoclassical sculpture on the mantelpiece in the study. Andrea's own-design checked linen covers an armchair from B&B Italia; behind it hangs a work by the 20th-century artist Alighiero Boetti.

BELOW Andrea's rainproof textiles protect the cushions on the terrace.
BOTTOM A plaster model of the façade of an 18th-century church sits on a small console table. The squared shape of the armchair is in keeping with Andrea's abiding taste for the geometrical.

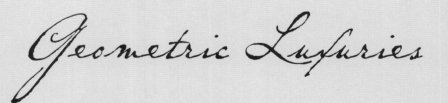

Geometric Luxuries

In the centre of Rome's ancient Campo Marzio quarter, on the narrow streets off the Via del Corso, are the city's most exclusive shops. It's here, at the top of a majestic 19th-century building, that the architect and interior designer Andrea Truglio lives and works. Curiously, Andrea once renovated and furnished this apartment for a client. With some surprise, he found himself moving into it 20 years later.

THIS PAGE At dawn and at dusk, the scents of bay, basil, rosemary and other aromatic herbs waft over an airy paradise offering spectacular views of the gardens of the Villa Borghese and Villa Medici, as well as the Santissima Trinità dei Monti, the church that crowns the Spanish Steps. The lacquered metal chairs are by Studio Truglio.

It amused Andrea to adapt a space already imprinted with his own aesthetic – a blend of the Neoclassical and the Rationalist style of the 1930s and 1940s – to his own needs. Now much more open, the apartment celebrates his way of life and his own vision. The feeling throughout is one of orderly luxury seasoned with a dash of irony.

That luxury begins in the communal entrance of the *palazzo*. Paved in travertine, the stone used in ancient Rome, it leads into a central courtyard that was once filled with the residents' private carriages. These days it is a charming garden from which a steel and glass lift whisks Andrea directly up and into his flat, a privilege he relishes.

Inside, the apartment is awash with light at all hours of the day, and the barely definable shades of earth and air find their way onto the walls, which vary from white to dove-grey. It all creates a neutral backdrop for the furniture Andrea designs, as well as for his impressive art collection. A work by Alberto di Fabio on rice paper brightens a white wall in the spare bedroom, and at right angles to it, on a petrol-coloured wall, is a piece by Domenico Bianchi.

The kitchen is as streamlined as the rest of the space, with white-lacquered units and an island. In the dining room, vintage steel chairs are paired with a long oak table supporting a sculpture by Francesco Ardini.

ABOVE The linen armchair and the two-tone lacquered chest of drawers are both Truglio designs. On the chest are positioned a black ceramic sculpture by Francesco Ardini and a lamp by Luceplan; a picture by David Tremlett hangs above. The sitting room can be glimpsed through the open doorway of the studio.

ABOVE A plaster model of Cellini's *Perseus*, realized in 1830 by Adamo Tadolini, stands on a white plinth. Beside it is a picture by Richard Woods. The floors and the door frames are travertine; the doors themselves are mirrored.

LEFT The interesting effects of this wall painting by Vicol Alexa helped to reshape a difficult rectilinear dining-room, infusing it with the rational geometry of Mondrian: a warm ochre band cuts through cooler tones of grey, white and black. Italian vintage chairs from the 1960s surround Francesco Ardini's tangled sculpture on the table, and a bi-coloured metal base supports a marble bust.

A living room and a study occupy a generous 100 square metres/1075 square feet in the centre of the apartment. Seating in the designer's preferred tones of grey and sand clusters around a large, low coffee table, and cylindrical occasional tables in lemon yellow and charcoal grey can be rearranged to interrupt static rhythms, or to splash the light around.

From the living room, a *scala a chiocciola,* or spiral staircase, winds up to reach guest accommodation in the 'super-attic', and on to the terrace. There, the colours of the sunset unite, as in a painting by Corot, to celebrate the timeless, melancholy beauty of the Eternal City.

ABOVE The square white coffee table and colourful cylindrical tables in the sitting room were all designed by the owner. A standard lamp by Luceplan lights up the vertical white stripe on the wall. The figure on the coffee table, a 1930s sculpture by Arno Breker, might easily have wandered off the sports field at Rome's Foro Italico.
RIGHT Andrea's collection of Neoclassical drawings is perfectly at home in the starkly elegant, black-and-white kitchen of his own design.

THIS PAGE In the sitting room, an elegant spiral staircase breaks up the straight lines of the furniture, rug and painting, and sweeps up to the guest accommodation on the top floor – and a roof terrace with breathtaking views of Rome.

THIS PAGE In the spare bedroom, two lamps by Arne Jacobsen for Louis Poulsen light up both sides of a bed designed by Truglio and dressed in brown, blue and yellow. To the left of the bed is a panel of concealed wardrobes.

ABOVE An antique Ashanti footstool crouches beneath a striking, nine-piece work by the artist Alberto di Fabio, whose bisecting lines interrupt the picture's organic forms.

ABOVE RIGHT Philippe Starck's horn-shaped lamp and a work by Domenico Bianchi stand against a blue-green wall. The 1940s rattan armchair is vintage Jean Michel Frank.

RIGHT A photo by Fiorenzo Niccoli keeps watch over the guest bed, which is covered with an ikat in Indian cotton. The athlete Apoxyomenos is the subject of the bronze Neoclassical sculpture at the end of the room, standing under a work by Daniele Puppi. On the nightstand is a Philippe Starck lamp.

Songs of Love and Death

Some of the most beautiful interiors in all of Italy can be found in its historic opera houses. With plush velvet seating, ornate, gilded balconies and magnificent chandeliers suspended from richly frescoed ceilings, they are the perfect settings for the tragedies and comedies enacted within their walls.

Like life, opera encompasses every gesture, every emotion, and Italians are absolutely devoted to it. Its stories of farce, revenge and disappointed love may seem exaggerated, but they replicate, albeit in grand form, the little dramas played out in everyday life.

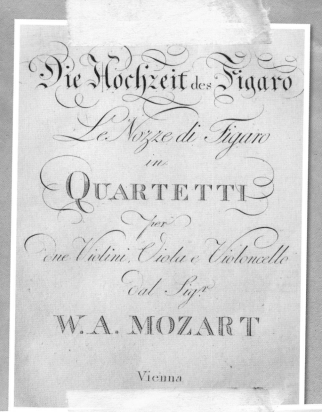

Il Teatro di San Cassiano, built in 1637 in Venice, was the first opera house, and Monteverdi was its star composer. By the end of the 1700s, it had been eclipsed by the ill-fated La Fenice, whose many misfortunes have themselves mimicked the twists and turns of operatic drama.

Milan's La Scala opened in 1778 with a performance by Antonio Salieri, Mozart's rival. And Mozart worked with an Italian librettist, Lorenzo da Ponte, on some of his best-loved operas: *The Marriage of Figaro*, *Don Giovanni* and *Così Fan Tutte*.

The 19th-century composers Rossini, Donizetti and Bellini revolutionized Italian opera with the melodic *bel canto* style, but it was Giuseppe Verdi who captured the heart of the newly unified nation with his grandly patriotic themes such as *Va, Pensiero* from the 1842 opera *Nabucco*. And the tragic operas of Puccini continue to pull at the heartstrings.

135

Although *Gnocchi alla Romana* share a wonderfully squidgy texture with the better known potato-based gnocchi, their chief ingredient is semolina. In this recipe, herbs and mustard have been included in the basic mix to add bite. Simple to make, these creamy discs are a great favourite with children of all ages.

Gnocchi alla Romana

1 litre/quart milk
250 g/1⅔ cups semolina
175 g/1¾ cups freshly
  grated Parmesan cheese
125 g/ 1 stick butter
2 medium egg yolks
1 tablespoon Dijon mustard
2 tablespoons chopped
  fresh sage, plus (optional)
  extra whole leaves to
  garnish
3 tablespoons chopped fresh
  flat leaf parsley
sea salt and freshly ground
  black pepper

circular biscuit cutter
ovenproof baking dish

Serves 4–6

Pour the milk into a saucepan and whisk in the semolina. Bring slowly to the boil, stirring all the time until it really thickens – about 10 minutes (it should be quite thick, like choux paste). Beat in half the Parmesan, half the butter, the egg yolks, mustard, sage and parsley. Add salt and pepper to taste.

Spread the mixture onto the lined baking sheet to a depth of 1.25 cm/½ inch. Let cool and set, about 2 hours.

Preheat the oven to 200°C (400°F) Gas 6. Cut the set mixture into circles with the biscuit cutter. Spread the chopped trimmings in the bottom of the ovenproof dish. Dot with some of the remaining butter and sprinkle with a little of the remaining Parmesan. Arrange the *gnocchi* shapes in a single layer over the trimmings. Dot with the remaining butter and Parmesan and scatter over a few sage leaves, if desired. Bake for 20–25 minutes until golden and crusty. Let stand for 5 minutes before serving.

The Edge of the World

Who can resist the pull of the unknown? Apulia, in the heel of Italy's boot-shaped island, seems to exist outside of time. Surrounded by the Adriatic and the Ionian seas, with the Gulf of Otranto lying to the south, it's an unspoiled region of bold landscapes, bright colours and distant horizons. For the Bolognese architect Marco Costanzi, it's the edge of the world, 'a place where the earth plunges into the sea and, in doing so, opens up the infinite'.

ABOVE LEFT Huddling at the edge of the property is a square hut constructed in a mixture of light-grey Lecce stone and pink stone, which matches the red earth of the region.

ABOVE RIGHT The eye barely distinguishes between the pale stone of this seating area and the cushions that soften its contours.

RIGHT Handmade stools crouch beneath the clean, straight lines of this monumental low table topped in steel. Plenty of firewood is stacked underneath a shelter of similar construction. The string of lights was designed by Fratelli Parisi.

THIS PAGE A simple ladder casts shadows to match the patterns of the stonework on this roof terrace (left). From the cool interior (below), one glimpses the fierce sun at the end of the enfilade; the pale tones of the straw hats and linen shirts are visually restful. Outside, a white path edged in local stone skirts a grove of ancient olive trees, their trunks deeply rooted in the region's red soil (below left).

It's here that Marco makes his second home, along with his wife Francesca, his son Ludovico and their dog Rua. It's not just a holiday home, but a retreat from life's excesses – its noise and the daily bombardment of imagery. Costanzi feels fortunate to have found this place with its unique atmosphere, one that allows him to work 'by subtraction', stripping out the inessentials and focusing on the eternals of land, sky and sea. Acquiring this property offered Costanzi the chance to practise a new kind of architecture.

Once a relatively small hunting lodge dating from around 1700, the structure was extended in the 1930s, and has, during its long history, functioned as an occasional shelter for olive-pickers at harvest time. By the time Marco bought it, the place had been abandoned for many years, so he had to redo it from the bottom up, installing heating, plumbing, floors, doors and windows.

Like many of the buildings in the province of Salento, the house was originally built with dry stone. Marco succeeded in preserving the

original layout while acknowledging all the practicalities of daily life. The building is articulated in a series of rooms, all at ground-floor level, each leading into another, without any imposed hierarchy; there are two bedrooms and two bathrooms. The kitchen, for example, is a passageway that connects the main living area with the outdoors; it opens onto an extensive terrace at ground level surrounded by olive trees. This kind of flow respects the house's original plan and is important to the way the family uses the space.

In keeping with his programme of subtraction, Marco opted for pure, refined lines, both inside and out. He conceived the project as a 'tactile and sensuous exploration of spaces and materials in a minimalist key, paying particular attention to the environment'. Spaces inside are huge and cavernous, in terms of their porportions and also as a result of their relative emptiness. Spartan furnishings are of straw, wood, stone and linen; there are no bright colours to compete with the rich colour of the earth or the silvery green of olive leaves. Walls are rendered in polished

THIS PAGE Linen drapes over the bare essentials concealed in this cupboard–wardrobe built into the fabric of the wall, with the beautiful masonry providing all the drama necessary. The curtain rod, equally unobtrusive, was fashioned from olive wood.

concrete, and plastered with a powder made of Lecce stone and limestone. They tone with the floors, themselves paved with stone from Lecce. The oldest part of the house, with its ancient wood-burning oven, has been opened up into an astonishing double-height living room, from where a sculptural, floating staircase climbs a bare wall to the mezzanine level and the bedrooms. Instead of partitioning the rooms, Marco has built walls to delineate the sleeping area from the washing area, equipped with a huge round showerhead, rustic stool and woven basket for toiletries. It's a short walk out onto a roof projecting over the olive grove. A guest bedroom is located in the former stables.

There is no garden as such. Instead, the centuries-old olive trees stand on roughly two and a half acres of red earth dotted with cactus and bordered by Mediterranean shrubs scenting the air with anise, myrtle, thyme, juniper, sage, rosemary and lavender. In a single concession to modernity, star-shaped installations by Fratelli Parisi twinkle throughout the property, both inside and out. It's as if they've died and gone to heaven, right here in Apulia.

THIS PAGE Doubling as a sleeping and study area, the mezzanine (top) fits comfortably under the high vaulting of the living-room ceiling, its lines forming a half-moon; it leads out to a projecting rooftop that looks over an olive orchard. A woven basket, pottery jug, leather briefcase and wooden stool gather together in a still life without cluttering the space (above). In the bathroom (right), a rather sculptural stone container for collecting olive oil has been reused as a basin, and a ladder serves as a towel rack.

*Open my heart and
you will see Graved
inside of it, 'Italy'*

Robert Browning

Open my heart and
you will see Graved
inside of it, 'Italy.'

Robert Browning

L'Olio di Oliva

In the first century AD, the Roman historian Pliny claimed that Italy had 'excellent olive oil at reasonable prices'. Not much has changed since then. Italy now produces around 22% of the world's olive oil, and while Florence, Siena and Lucca may each have earned the title *città dell'olio*, or oil city, most of the country's olive oil comes from the southern regions of Puglia and Calabria.

Olive harvesting begins in October and continues into early December. Although it is possible to harvest olives using a machine, they sustain less damage if they are gathered in the traditional way, beating the branches by hand with a flexible rod and collecting the fruit in nets spread over the ground beneath the trees.

The most highly prized oil is, naturally, *olio extravergine di oliva*, the result of the first cold pressing of the fruit; it must not contain more than 0.8% acidity. *Olio di oliva vergine* can have an acidity level of up to 2%. *Olio di oliva raffinato*, with an acidity level of 0.3%, is produced by treating virgin olive oil of high acidity with filtering agents such as charcoal; its taste can then be adjusted by adding small amounts of superior oils.

Umbrian olive oil is fruity and full flavoured with a hint of almonds, while oil from the Marche is rather herbal. Some of the finest olive oil, spicy and green, is Sicilian. Puglian oil is long-lasting and good for cooking, while Calabria's is grassy, with hints of artichoke. Tuscan olive oil is very smooth, and oil from Liguria is sweet, mild and flowery.

Like *Insalata Caprese* (see pages 112–113) this delectable cake comes from the island of Capri. It is sinfully rich, and can be eaten by anyone with a wheat allergy since it is made with ground almonds rather than flour. Serve with a cup of strong espresso.

Torta Caprese

200 g/1 cup granulated
   sugar

4 medium eggs, separated

200 g/1¾ sticks butter,
   melted and cooled

200 g/7 oz. dark/bittersweet
   chocolate, finely chopped

250 g/1⅔ cups whole
   blanched almonds, finely
   chopped

2 tablespoons Strega liqueur
   (optional)

icing/confectioners' sugar,
   for dusting

23-cm/9-inch springform
   cake pan, lightly buttered
   and base-lined

Serves 8–10

Preheat the oven to 180°C (350°F) Gas 4.

Beat the sugar and egg yolks together until light and fluffy.

Stir in the cooled melted butter and then the chocolate and almonds. Add the Strega at this point, if using.

In a clean bowl, whisk the egg whites until firm. Fold them lightly but thoroughly into the almond mixture until they are fully incorporated. Spoon the mixture into the prepared tin and cook for about 30 minutes (the cake will be slightly squidgy in the centre). Remove from the oven and leave to cool in the tin.

Dust with icing/confectioners' sugar and serve.

La Sicilia 4

Sicily

These crispy golden balls are the apotheosis of leftovers, in which last night's *risotto* and cheese or *ragù* are combined to make the perfect cocktail snack. Popular all over Sicily as street food, *arancini di riso* are generally plum-sized. If you're making the rice up especially, be sure to overcook it so that it will be sticky; the mixture should be thick.

Arancini di Riso

75 g/6 tablespoons unsalted butter
1 onion, finely chopped
150 ml/⅔ cup dry white wine
275 g *risotto* rice, preferably arborio
900 ml/1 quart good-quality vegetable stock or light chicken stock, heated until just boiling
8 saffron threads or ¼ teaspoon powdered saffron
25 g/¼ cup freshly grated Parmesan cheese
1 small egg
about 250 g/1 cup leftover *ragù*
sea salt and freshly ground black pepper
vegetable oil, for deep-frying

coating
100 g/⅔ cup plain/all-purpose flour
2 large eggs, beaten
125 g/1 cup dried white breadcrumbs

Serves 4-6

Melt the butter in a large, heavy saucepan and add the onion. Cook gently for 10 minutes until soft and golden but not browned. Pour in the wine and boil hard until reduced and almost disappeared. Stir in the rice and coat with the butter and wine. Add a ladle of stock and the saffron and simmer, stirring until absorbed. Continue adding the stock, ladle by ladle, until all the stock has been absorbed. The rice should be very tender, thick and golden. (This should take about 20 minutes.)

Taste and season well with salt and pepper, then stir in the Parmesan. Lightly whisk the egg and beat into the risotto. Spread out on a plate and let cool completely, about 1 hour. Take 1 tablespoon cold risotto and, with damp hands, spread out in the palm of one hand. Mound a small teaspoon of meat *ragù* in the centre. Take another tablespoon of risotto and set over the *ragù* to enclose it completely. Carefully roll and smooth in your hands to form a perfect round ball (or form into a cone shape with a rounded end). Continue until all the risotto and filling has been used.

To make the coating, put the flour on a plate, the beaten eggs in a shallow dish and the breadcrumbs in a shallow bowl. Roll the *arancini* first in the flour, then in the egg and finally in the breadcrumbs until evenly coated. At this stage, they can be covered and left in the refrigerator for up to 1 day.

Heat the oil in a deep-fryer or wok until a crumb will sizzle immediately – 180°C (350°F). Fry a few *arancini* at a time for 3–5 minutes until deep golden. Drain on kitchen paper/paper towels, sprinkle with salt and serve immediately (or keep warm in a low oven for up to 15 minutes).

Note: For vegetarians, instead of the meat *ragù* filling, use 100 g/3½ oz. finely chopped mozzarella, 4 sun-dried tomatoes in oil, drained and finely chopped, and a few finely chopped fresh basil leaves.

Palace of Dreams

With five children, fashion designer Luisa
Beccaria and her husband need quite a bit
of space. Their *palazzo* at Borgo del
Castelluccio allows them to spread out
comfortably, and offers the perfect escape
from daily life in Milan. Although it had
been in her husband's family for centuries,
Luisa first saw it during one almond
harvest, and immediately fell in love.

LEFT Castelluccio is the perfect embodiment of
the elegance of Sicilian architecture. The straight
lines of its façade are enhanced by classical
architraves and broken only by the two bell towers
attached to the property's private chapel.
ABOVE Citrus, almond, pomegranate, cypress and
olive are some of the wide variety of trees and
plants growing on the estate, which lies between
the mountains and the sea.

ABOVE AND RIGHT The Sicilian sun can be fierce, so it's good to have a few sheltered spots to escape from the blaze. Here (above), a bench is placed in the shadow cast by an overhanging arch and bright pink bougainvillaea plants, which are native to the region. Huge urns, once used for storing olive oil, were rescued and placed in a cool, vaulted storeroom off the central courtyard (right). Beside them is a 19th-century bench, painted according to local tradition. When the property was still a working farm, such storerooms were packed with agricultural equipment and produce.

ABOVE The estate's former stables have been converted into a tranquil relaxation area around the swimming pool. Wisteria drips from the pergola and loose curtains sway with the breeze. Tired swimmers can take to the shade, or just sit comfortably on the plump mattresses cushioning these wooden benches.

Hidden between the Hyblaean Mountains and the coast near Syracuse, the *borgo*, or village, includes an 18th-century *palazzo*, a chapel and assorted agricultural buildings. It had, at the close of the 19th century, been styled by a famous French decorator. Then, like Sleeping Beauty, it was left slumbering for more than 60 years before waking up to its prince – in this case, a genuine one. Luisa's aristocratic husband Lucio Bonaccorsi had always shunned the property,

finding its location too isolated. But with the help of a close friend, the painter Teddy Millington-Drake, Luisa convinced him to restore the *borgo* as a gift for their children – and to Sicily itself.

It wasn't a project for the faint-hearted. The entire complex was crumbling and the roof had caved in. Work began on the lower storey of the central wing, which once housed farm animals. It was incorporated into the rest of

LEFT Painted farm wagons such as these three are a traditional sight in Sicily. Though Castelluccio is still a working farm, these wagons are now safely preserved in an outbuilding.
ABOVE Cool tones predominate in one of the many sitting rooms. The same handwoven Indian linen covers each chair and sofa.

BELOW LEFT In the dining room, the predominantly white palette is touched with shades of blue ranging from ice-cool to lilac and deep cobalt. An antique dresser holds family china.
OPPOSITE From a raised dais in the former stables, you can glimpse the garden through a rose-covered doorway while lying on soft cushions.

the house, which embraces a cobbled courtyard. Teddy Millington-Drake took charge of the planting outside — only two pomegranate trees were still alive in the walled garden — and Luisa and her husband saw to the interiors. When Teddy sadly died, Luisa continued his work in the gardens.

Work continues to this day, with new projects continually presenting themselves, either of necessity or due to a brainwave of Luisa's. Yet the experience of walking into the house is unforgettable. Light bounces off walls tinted with shades of white and blue. 'I did try to add a few touches of colour by mixing powdered tints with whitewash. Otherwise, when evening falls, pure white turns to grey, and the effect can be cold,' says Luisa. With gilded white furniture and gauze curtains that bloom in the wind, these dreamy interiors recall not only the lost way of life in Giuseppe Tomasi di Lampedusa's historical novel *The Leopard,* but also the romantic gossamer dresses of Luisa's eponymous fashion house.

Back outside, a climb up the watchtower is rewarded with views of the countryside, where cypresses mingle with lemon, orange and almond trees. After a visit to Castelluccio, you might find yourself dreaming.

To have seen Italy without having seen Sicily is to have seen nothing, for Sicily is the clue to everything.

Goethe

To have seen Italy without
having seen Sicily is to have
seen nothing, for Sicily is the
clue to everything.   Goethe

La Cucina Siciliana

Sicilian food is a tantalizing mixture of flavours, many of them recognizably Italian, others intriguingly exotic. The ingredients of a succession of diverse occupying cultures, including the Greeks, North Africans, French and Spanish, have infused this fabulously rich and varied cuisine.

Seafood and fish, especially tuna, are central to the island's menu. Equally important is the humble aubergine/eggplant, which appears in a wide variety of classic dishes such as *caponata*, a rich savoury stew containing pine nuts, whole olives and occasionally even chocolate (see pages 164–165); first courses such as *pasta alla Norma*, which also features ricotta; and the strange and exciting *lucumie*, sweet pastries stuffed with aubergine, almond butter, honey and cinnamon.

Arab and Spanish influences can be detected in the refreshing *insalata di arance*, a salad of sliced oranges, fennel bulb, black olives and onions often served at the end of a meal. And on the western side of the island, in Trapani, ground almonds and tomatoes are blended together in a delicious *pesto alla Trapanese* that's a far cry from the traditional basil and pine nut *pesto* of mainland Liguria.

Street food is hugely popular in Palermo, where crispy *panelle* have been eaten since the Middle Ages. These flat savoury fritters, made of *farina di ceci*, or chickpea flour, are deep-fried and sprinkled with pepper and perhaps a few drops of lemon juice. Plump *arancini*, little balls of cooked rice folded around a filling of meat or cheese (see pages 152–153), *timballini di pasta*, or crispy fried pasta, and *pasticcino,* a sweet pastry with various fillings, are just some of the delights that can be found at fried-food kiosks – or *friggitorie* – all over Palermo.

In origin a summer dish, *caponata* (*capunata* in Sicilian dialect) is an exotic combination of sweet and sour, with aubergine in the starring role. The name may be Catalan, or it may have developed from the word for sailors' bars, *caupone*. Wherever it came from, *caponata* is velvety and unctuous and often includes pine nuts and raisins, occasionally even chocolate, like Mexican mole sauce. There are variations based on seafood, such as a Palermo recipe with octopus, but most commonly it consists simply of cubed aubergine, tomato and celery with the addition of vinegar and sugar. Make ahead, as the flavour improves with age. Like revenge, this is a dish best served cold – or perhaps at room temperature!

Caponata

4 medium aubergines/
  eggplant, cut into bite-
  sized cubes
4 tablespoons olive oil
1 onion, chopped
2 celery stalks, sliced
12 very ripe large tomatoes,
  coarsely chopped, or
  600 g/21 oz. canned
  chopped tomatoes
1–2 tablespoons salted
  capers, rinsed well
100 g/⅔ cup best green
  olives, pitted
2 tablespoons red wine
  vinegar, or to taste
2 teaspoons sugar, or
  to taste
vegetable oil, for deep-frying
sea salt

to serve
200 g/7 oz. fresh ricotta
  cheese
toasted chopped almonds
freshly chopped fresh flat
  leaf parsley

Serves 6

Put the aubergines/eggplant in a colander, sprinkle with salt and let drain for 30 minutes.

Heat the olive oil in a saucepan and add the onion and celery. Cook for 5 minutes until softened but not browned, then add the tomatoes and cook for 15 minutes until pulpy. Add the capers, olives, vinegar and sugar to the sauce and cook for a further 15 minutes.

Rinse the aubergine/eggplant cubes and pat dry with kitchen paper/paper towels.

Heat the vegetable oil in a deep-fryer or wok to 190°C (375°F), add the cubes in batches and fry until deep golden brown. This may take some time, but cook them thoroughly, because undercooked aubergine/eggplant is unpleasant. Alternatively, toss the cubes in olive oil, spread in a roasting tin and roast at 200°C (400°F) Gas 6 for 20 minutes or until well browned and tender. Drain well.

Stir the aubergines/eggplant into the sauce. Taste and adjust the seasoning (adding more sugar or vinegar to taste to balance the flavours). Set aside for at least 30 minutes or overnight to develop the flavours before serving. Serve warm or at room temperature (never refrigerator-cold) in a shallow bowl and top with the ricotta, almonds and parsley.

THIS PAGE AND OPPOSITE
The pool and garden area is completely new, and still being developed. Dry-stone walls were restored or built from scratch, the earth was resurfaced and native plants and shrubs reinstated. The pool itself was created by digging straight into the rock; beyond it are the arid fields where farm labourers once toiled. All the houses in the area are built of stone found in these fields, and compacted earth can still be seen in the natural holes that pit the stones used to construct this *masseria*.

Artist's Retreat

The artist Velasco Vitali comes from an artistic family near Lake Como, where he still lives. When a friend and gallery owner invited him to exhibit in Comiso, a small town in Sicily, Velasco rented a house in the Hyblaean Mountains, a region he had never visited. What began as a busman's holiday ended up changing his life. Even the house he stayed in unexpectedly became his own.

LEFT AND RIGHT Simple curtains stretched over iron frames provide shade in the *baglio*, or courtyard.
BELOW AND OPPOSITE From the dining area, a floating staircase in cement climbs to the loft and guest bedroom. Floors were paved with local *pietra di Comiso* or, as here, slabs of *pietra pece*, a type of local limestone impregnated with fossils and mineral oil. For months after they are first excavated and laid, a faint smell of diesel lingers. After a while, the smell fades, as does the colour; with waxing, it reveals greenish-black veins and transparent white lines.

For Velasco, the trip down south meant the discovery of a totally new world. Compared with the cooler, gentler lakeside landscape and geography that he knew so well, he found the southeast of Sicily to be a region of tremendous contrasts. And although Velasco wasn't looking for a house at the time, he immediately felt that 'something there was waiting for me. The encounter with the land and house was a real surprise. I felt the need to be in that place for long periods of time, even though it was little more than a stable.'

Velasco bought the property only when the owners phoned him to say that someone else had put down a deposit on it, and it was time for him to leave. No one could say exactly how old it was, but the nucleus of this *masseria*, a fortified manorial farmhouse typical of the region, is at least three or four hundred years old. The former dwellings of the landowner and the peasants are grouped around a square central courtyard paved with limestone. At its centre is a huge cistern – as big as a room – carved deep into the rock in order to collect and store the winter rain the dry earth so badly needed for crops. Today, the cistern is used to store water for the garden.

In recognition of the two votive niches over its entrance, the house was named Le Edicole – 'the niches' – and its renovation evolved just like one of Velasco's sculptures, with the same respect and understanding for the expressive potential of the medium. Under the guidance of the architect Arturo Montanelli and with the invaluable help of Vincenzo Agosta, every part of the *masseria* was altered, as if it had been torn from the earth, cleaned, refurbished from top to bottom and then replaced. Every stone was repositioned. In the courtyard, the depth of the paving stones allowed them to be cut into three, and the new pieces of stone were used to pave a part of it that had formerly only been compacted earth, just as it had been when carriages rattled over the ground.

Beneath the roofs, with their wooden beams and clay tiles, there is now, as in the past, a suspended ceiling made of bamboo canes secured with iron bands and a layer of plaster. This traditional insulation technique provides a type of natural air-conditioning, allowing hot air to escape outside and keeping the house cool during the summers – an important consideration in a place where temperatures routinely reach 40°C/104°F.

A visit to the house, Velasco says, might just as well begin with the bathrooms as with the courtyard. The bathtub in his studio was dug out of the solid rock, and its zinc plumbing has been left unconcealed. The shower's water jets are separated by one of his paintings, which shows two men carrying an upturned boat over their heads,

and the sink was carved from stone from a nearby field. The other bathrooms in the house are of a similar design, though their flooring varies from simple *pietra pece* to white limestone. The internal doors are made of zinc, their lines simple and formal.

There are two kitchens, one for breakfast and one for family meals. The breakfast kitchen, in Velasco's studio, comes equipped with a massive sink, formerly used for preserving olives, while the work surface was made from stone excavated from the pool area. Zinc-plated iron and planks left behind by the builders were used to build the open shelving. A large round reel, found on the beach by the artist and his friends, now serves as a table. In the family kitchen, with its long, thick metal work surface, cooking

utensils dangle from the wall in a kind of culinary installation. The kitchen table was designed and built by Velasco, who also restored the rest of the furniture. 'I must admit that we sometimes pick things up off the street, like the small table in the sitting room,' he confesses.

In fact, most of the furniture throughout the house was either designed and built or restored by Velasco and his companion, Cristina. Velasco particularly enjoyed restoring a Sicilian bed bought for only a few euros, with panels originally painted to look like real marble.

Each of the four bedrooms has its own distinct personality. Velasco and Cristina share one that's completely open, with a large window that looks out onto the olive groves below. The room of their sons, Rocco and Oliviero,

LEFT AND OPPOSITE
In the breakfast kitchen in Velasco's studio, a basin once used for pickling olives has become a sink (opposite); the work surface alongside it is a piece of stone dug from the hole for the swimming pool. Open shelving was constructed using bits of wood left around during reconstruction, and the kitchen's simplicity is on a par with the artist's culinary talents. Seen left is the family kitchen, equipped with every modern convenience necessary for family life. Velasco designed and built the table himself.

ABOVE A rectangular stone sink embodies the linear approach to the redesign and reconstruction of this ancient farmhouse. Every stone was cleaned and repositioned.

RIGHT The artist's bathroom was literally dug into the rock in the house's former stables, and its small sink was carved from a stone found in the fields outside. The floors are laid with *pietra di Comiso*, a local white stone with light-grey veining like graphite markings. This idea of bare, excavated stone was carried through to the other bathrooms, which all have doors of polished zinc.

ABOVE Soft light filters through triangular openings of a stone panel above the bed in the open-plan master bedroom; the holes were once filled with roosting pigeons. The room, with its double-height ceilings, was formerly the hayloft and now enjoys a view of the olive grove outside. Velasco's painting of sheets hangs halfway up one wall.

is almost monastic in its simplicity, with plain iron beds designed by their father. The guestroom is the most private space, and has windows framing a gorgeous view of the swimming pool. A floating cement staircase leads from the ground floor right up to the loft, where further bedrooms are lit by the same small triangular openings seen in the wall of the master bedroom. Velasco's studio holds only a bed, a curtain and two stone niches, making it the most spartan. Two tiny zinc windows, like those of a *camera oscura*, allow light into the room.

Throughout the house, Velasco's artwork is a reminder of the materials used during the renovation, when he laboured for long periods of time outdoors, putting into his work some of the objects he found in the surrounding fields. 'The energy of this place, which originates in the land, has fundamentally altered the way I work,' he says. Two dogs sculpted in tar sit mutely in the courtyard, as if cowed by the family hound, Asia. Beyond them, the Sicilian countryside stretches undisturbed for miles, dotted with native citrus, olive and carob trees.

Sicilian Sweet Treats

How can you not fall in love with an island whose people gnaw on Virgins' Breasts and the Bones of the Dead? It is the Arabs we have to thank for introducing to Sicily the pistachios, lemons, oranges, dates, sugar and spices on which their pastries and desserts are now based.

A favourite with Sicilians and foreigners alike, *Cannoli* are little pipes of crisp, spiced pastry oozing with sugary cream containing ricotta, chocolate or pistachio and topped with sweetened peel. Other indulgent pastries include *Zeppole* or *Sfinci di San Giuseppe*. Baked rather than fried, these doughnut-like cream-filled goodies are named after Joseph, the patron saint of pastry chefs. The aptly named *Trionfo di Gola,* the 'triumph of gluttony', is a rich and elaborate dessert that originated in Palermo. Its sugary sponge cake is thickly layered with pistachio preserves, milk pudding and marzipan, and drenched in tangerine liqueur.

Some Sicilian sweet treats have a rather macabre bent, such as *Minni di Virgini*, or 'St Agatha's breasts'. The patron saint of Catania, Agatha was tortured in prison by having her breasts cut off. Little iced cakes filled with squash preserves and crowned with a glacé cherry are eaten in her honour every February. Then there are the oval biscuits named *Occhi di Santa Lucia*, or 'eyes of St Lucy'. Legend has it that the saint's eyes were gouged out before her execution, and to celebrate her feast day in December and May, the Pasticceria Marciante in Siracusa created these little biscuits stuffed with marzipan, golden raisins and orange zest. And the gruesomely named *Ossa di Morto* – rock-hard and pale biscuits shaped like bones – show up in pastry shops for All Souls' Day.

Anyone with a passion for marzipan will enjoy dainty *Frutta di Martorana*. Legend has it that, one Easter, nuns at the convent of the Martorana in Palermo decorated barren trees with marzipan sweets to celebrate the Archbishop's arrival. Completely hoodwinked, he believed that the colourful *frutta* grew from miraculous trees.

CANNOLO
Siciliano
€ 2,50 L'UNO

A lemon is edible sunlight. Tremendously versatile, its sharp clean flavour shouts 'Summer!' and sparks savoury and sweet dishes alike. On the island of Capri, its glossy dark green leaves are wrapped around fresh buffalo mozzarella, which is then grilled. Sicilian lemons are just as big and beautiful, and here, they are plumped out with an icy, sour–sweet sorbetto. If possible, decorate with a blossom.

Sorbetto al Limone

300 g/1½ cups granulated
    sugar
finely grated zest and juice
    of 6 unwaxed lemons, plus
    6 medium, even-sized
    lemons
finely grated zest and juice
    of 1 unwaxed orange

an ice-cream maker

Serves 6

Put the sugar and 600 ml/1 pint water in a saucepan with the lemon and orange zest. Bring slowly to the boil and boil rapidly for 3–4 minutes. Remove from the heat, and let cool. Meanwhile, strain the citrus juices into a bowl. When the syrup is cold, strain into the bowl of juice. Chill. When cold, churn in an ice-cream maker, following the manufacturer's instructions until frozen.

Meanwhile, cut the tops off the remaining 6 lemons and shave a little off the base of each so that it will stand up. Scoop out the insides, squeeze and keep the juice for another time. Put the lemon shells in the freezer. When the sorbet is frozen, fill the lemon shells and set the tops back on. Replace in the freezer until needed. Soften in the refrigerator for 10–15 minutes before serving.

Set in Stone

Tucked deep inside the city of Modica is an exotic house bought by an architect and her husband from Piedmont, in northern Italy, in 2010. The couple named their new home Zara Zabara, a phrase taken from a novel by Andrea Camilleri, the creator of Inspector Montalbano. In dialect, it means 'Everything changes, because nothing changes', and it was a phrase that seemed to summarize the restoration process and the effort that went into preserving the unique spirit of the place while adapting it to modern life and standards of comfort.

THIS PAGE This sun-trap terrace has become the centre of the owners' social life and strongly influenced their decision to buy the property. Paved with tiles from Caltagirone made to a design by Viviana Haddad, it overlooks the city, yet because the house is located in a traffic-free zone, it is wonderfully peaceful.

From the Middle Ages until a few decades ago, cave dwellings honeycombed the hills around Modica. With façades visible from the outside, they can be surprisingly extensive, incorporating 'invisible' rooms that were dug deep into the rocks, originally without tools. The result is a type of vernacular Sicilian architecture combined with features you might find in a *riad*.

As someone who restores old houses professionally, Marta Bassotto knew what she was getting into. So she consulted a local architect, Viviana Haddad, whose work she had seen while staying in the area. Haddad planned to create the Bassottos' dream house by bringing this ancient

OPPOSITE The owners enjoy cooking in their sleek kitchen. Patterned Sicilian tiles provide the splashback at a sink with taps/faucets by Fantini. The dining table was made to design and rests on flooring in *pietra pece*, a natural black stone.

LEFT AND ABOVE Made of laminated sheet metal, the kitchen cabinet doors (left) hide modern appliances. Cushioned stone seats (above) evoke an Arab flavour. The original shop counter was restored, and the pendant light in the far corner is vintage.

183

RIGHT Each of the floors in the house was separate when the owners bought it; not one of them communicated with another. A steel stairway now connects all three of them, its white banister creating intriguing geometries against the black floor and steps.
BELOW Much of the furniture in the house was bought from local antiques shops. These beautiful iron headboards date from the 1800s.

cave back to life, restoring its charm and opening up a dialogue between its past and its present. To achieve this, she brought all of Sicily's colours, light and traditional building materials into play, and visited the building site daily.

The house was initially uninhabitable, with three separate levels that did not connect. To make things more difficult, it is located in a section of the city accessible only by foot. So it's not surprising that the structural work lasted for two years and required all the local expertise the couple could call upon. Additions to the house were prohibited since Modica is UNESCO protected, and building work is governed by strict environmental regulations. The internal space, however, was entirely reconfigured. On the ground floor, which faces the via Cartellone, there had once been a small grocer's and haberdashery store serving the neighbouring residents. During the restoration, they kept finding odd buttons and small haberdashery items, packets of coffee and cocoa. None of this was wasted: eventually, they used the shop counter inside the house, which locals still recognize as *la putìa*, the old grocery.

Only traditional materials were used during the reconstruction, and these included whitewash, clay and *cocciopesto*, a type of mortar made with brick or pottery fragments mixed with lime and sand. The floors were laid with local stone and traditional-coloured cement tiles from the early 20th century. The original sloping roof was thatched with reeds and cork, while the guttering and downpipes were made of terracotta. Internal doors were turned into cupboards and wardrobes. All the plumbing and electricals, including underfloor heating, are more or less hidden.

THIS PAGE There is something of the *hammam* about the ground-floor bathroom, with its rough-hewn walls, huge showerhead and long, tasselled cotton towels. Originally a well, *la cisterna* has been stylishly modernized with taps/faucets by Fantini, vintage Italian lighting and a basin fashioned from reclaimed stone. The uneven ceiling is natural rock coated in traditional plaster, or *cocciopesto*. The period furniture, including the wooden towel rack, is Italian.

In *la putìa*, the old store on the ground floor, original vaulting was restored with clay plaster and coloured tiles were set into the floor. The owners call the first floor *le cannette* after the reeds that were used to repair the roof. As on the ground floor, so on this one: the flooring is in the traditional *cementine*, or coloured tiles. *La grotta*, the cave, is also on the first floor, and it's a room that was completely dug out of the rock. It's now plastered with *cocciopesto* and

clay; the flooring, too, is *cocciopesto*. The same material was used in the ground-floor bathroom, *la cisterna*, which started its life as a well in the 16th century.

The kitchen can be found on the second floor of the house. It forms part of an open-plan area that includes the dining room and sitting room. All the modern technology – washing machine, dishwasher and such – is built under a counter of stonework coated with stylish acrylic resin.

The house is extremely peaceful and silent, even though it's only 118 steps away from Corso Umberto, Modica's busy main street. Now a much-loved holiday home for Marta and Domenico, Zara Zabara offers them a peaceful haven that they can share with their dogs, Virgola and Gilda, and with friends. Living there, they say, is plunging into the 'once upon a time', and choosing this place was 'a crazy indulgence of the heart'.

ABOVE The owners furnished each room with a mixture of Sicilian antiques, such as this desk and chair, and specially designed pieces. The heavy wooden doors were made by local carpenters; the curtains and bedding are cotton.

ABOVE LEFT A local saint watches over quiet slumbers in the ground-floor bedroom, called *la putìa*, or the grocers, to commemorate its history as a shop. The ceiling lamp is vintage, and the elaborately worked iron bedheads are 19th-century Sicilian painted in a soft grey.

The Architecture of Sicily

The architecture of Sicily is playful, elegant and theatrical. But things might have been entirely different, for in 1693 a devastating earthquake decimated at least 45 cities. The unique style that grew from the rubble during an extensive programme of reconstruction has become known as the Sicilian Baroque.

Noto is perhaps the most celebrated of all the 18th-century new towns that cluster in the southeastern area of the island. An ethereal, golden light haloes the entire town, and while the faithful ascend a vast bank of steps to pray in the domed cathedral, only a short distance away, *putti* and mythological beasts cavort from the stone balconies of the Palazzo Nicolaci di Villadorata in an effort to ward off evil spirits.

Nearby Syracuse was once a powerful Greek city-state. Its historical centre, the island of Ortigia, boasts one of the most beautiful cathedrals in all of Sicily. Doric columns, originally part of an ancient temple dedicated to Athena, have been incorporated into its structure, and it faces, along with Palazzo Beneventano, a splendid set-piece Baroque piazza.

Often seen in background scenes of the fictional Sicilian detective series *Montalbano*, Ragusa Ibla is the perfect foil to crime, ornate caryatids and grotesques watching from the balconies of its *palazzi*, and saints teetering atop the church of San Giorgio on scrolls shaped like cinnamon buns.

As if earthquakes were not enough, the volcanic eruptions of Mount Etna have repeatedly razed the city of Catania. Yet its impressive creamy-white *palazzi*, seemingly outlined in shadows, have been reconstructed from the very lava that once destroyed it.

A charming legend features the 13th-century king Frederick II who, while out hunting, encountered a farmer making ricotta and asked for some. Pouring hot ricotta over bread, he advised his men to eat theirs with a spoon or risk leaving it all behind. This light, lemony *torta* makes eating ricotta a lot easier.

Torta di Ricotta

pastry
175 g/1½ sticks butter, softened
50 g/¼ cup granulated sugar
1 medium egg yolk
250 g/2 cups plain/all-purpose flour, plus extra for dusting

ricotta filling
500 g/2 cups ricotta cheese
250 g/1 cup mascarpone cheese
200 g/1 cup granulated sugar
3 medium eggs, beaten
grated zest and freshly squeezed juice of 2 large unwaxed lemons
icing/confectioners' sugar, for dusting

23-cm/9-inch tart pan with removeable base

Serves 6-8

First make the pastry. Beat the butter and sugar together until smooth. Add the egg yolk and beat again until thoroughly mixed. Stir in the flour and work the mixture lightly until it forms a smooth but not sticky dough. Divide the dough in half and freeze one portion to use later.

Roll out the dough on a lightly floured work surface and use to line the tart tin. Chill for 30 minutes if time allows.

Preheat the oven to 180°C (350°F) Gas 4 while you make the filling.

Beat the ricotta and mascarpone together until very smooth and light. Add the granulated sugar, eggs and lemon zest and juice. Beat again until everything is thoroughly combined. Pour the mixture into the pastry case and bake for about 45 minutes until the filling is set. Remove from the oven and leave to cool in the tin. Dust with icing/confectioners' sugar and serve.

I sometimes feel a languishment
For skies Italian.

John Keats

John Keats

LEFT An ornate pillow rests on an antique wooden *sgabello*, or stool, and a *comò*, or dresser, topped with traditional grey-veined marble, hosts a carved crucifix. The photographs are the work of the artist Loredana Longo.

OPPOSITE Mariella loves this foyer with its original tiled flooring, 18th-century Sicilian bench and 19th-century oval table. The house is filled with old mirrors, which become sparkly with old age; she hopes to do the same.

A View of the Harbour

When a friend lent her a neglected apartment in the centre of Palermo, Mariella jumped at the chance to roost there while she did up her main property. It would be, for her, a 'house in waiting'. Even though it was painted 'a horrid peach–salmon' and had the stale smell of having been closed up for too many years, Mariella could see beyond the decay to its good bones and the wonderful original cement-tile flooring.

Having lived in Sydney, Australia, for the first 36 years of her life, working as a lawyer and then as a florist, Mariella came to Palermo for a year to explore her Sicilian roots and learn Italian. But she ended up lingering, and now she shares her flat with her two-year-old daughter.

The apartment is on an upper floor of a 19th-century *palazzo*, with views of Palermo's harbour. There are high ceilings with stucco mouldings, French doors and marble balconies, all of which give the flat a sense of light and space.

Mariella wanted first of all to restore a sense of freshness to the place, so she banished the nasty salmon colour in favour of bright white; the bathrooms and kitchen were regrouted. She then began to add selected items of her own furniture, most of which was in storage. Little by little, however, more pieces crept in until, she admits, most of her substantive pieces and artwork had settled there with her.

There is a continuity between the age of the building and Mariella's personal style, which sees dark furniture set

against white walls and mixed with mirrors and glass, a combination that balances beautifully and prevents the space from feeling heavy or cluttered. Many of her belongings have been found in and about Palermo and adapted. Her tables are a case in point, and have been put together from reclaimed objects, including an industrial wooden cog. She has also created a screen in her sitting room from three antique panels taken from the painted ceiling of an old Sicilian *palazzo*. Mariella believes 'an interior should reflect

ABOVE LEFT AND RIGHT French doors in the double sitting room let in fresh air from a balcony facing the sea; Mariella takes her coffee there, with her plants for company. This double-space living area is full of the texture the designer loves, with wood, glass and textiles mingled together. A passion for rescued objects found Mariella fashioning a table from a huge old industrial wooden cog. On top of it, a tall stem of wild fennel lords it over four curious bone candlesticks, a lamp and a bell jar.

the personality of those who inhabit the space', and that personality should be guided by design, not buried under it. For her, texture is what links it all together, and her own-design kilims and floor coverings, produced for the Viennese firm Oritop, add drama and richness to her home.

Along with carefully chosen antiques, contemporary art is a huge presence. The photographs in the main sitting room are by the Sicilian artist Loredana Longo, who has created explosion installations and photographed the remains. Monique Lovering's paintings and drawings are framed identically, yet hung in unlikely groupings.

As someone who loves to cook, Mariella considers a kitchen 'an open zone that communicates with living areas'. The original one here, however, seemed sited in a location from another era, when servants prepared food and brought it to the table in a more formal room. The space has now

ABOVE Why hide lovely kitchen utensils away in cupboards? A framed piece of fabric – Chinese silk with a calligraphy font – provides an exotic splashback; at floor level, a cleverly placed mirror extends this small space.
RIGHT Perfectly positioned for sea-gazing is this chaise longue in

black-and-white fabric. On the wall are two works by New Zealand artist Monique Lovering.
OPPOSITE Floor coverings, often a decorative afterthought, can transform a space. On the floor here is a kilim woven to the owner's own design in undyed New Zealand wool.

been shaped into a compact galley style with metal and marble, where the tools of the trade are all visible.

Rather to the amusement of everyone concerned, this flat, once a neglected rental property, has been so completely transformed by Mariella that the friend who lent it to her plans to move back in when Mariella moves out. The same friend has since learned that her father and his siblings were all born there. 'The fact that she has discovered something of her own past in this apartment has been an additional pleasure for us all.'

ABOVE In the intimate space of the flat's one bathroom, old mirrors mingle with 18th-century *acquerelli*, or watercolours, of noble children and pets. A fabric shower curtain designed by the owner is backed with plastic; a kilim adds a sumptuous touch. **ABOVE RIGHT** The long entrance hall connects the bedroom with the main living area.

THIS PAGE AND OPPOSITE BELOW In the bedroom, an antique mirror has been turned into an unusual nightstand, while a traditional painted door panel leans against a white backdrop. The owner's kilims dress the floor, and the bed is clothed in rich, earthy tones.

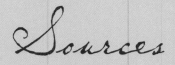

Sources

UK SOURCES

ITALIAN ANTIQUES AND CONTEMPORARY FURNISHINGS

Anton & K
1–2 High Street
Winchcombe
Gloucestershire GL54 5LJ
01242 602 644
www.antonandk.co.uk
Italian and continental furniture and decorative objects.

Architrave Antiques
Unit 44, The Vinery
Arundel Road
Poling, Arundel
West Sussex BN18 9PY
01903 882146
www.architraveantiques.co.uk
Architectural antiques.

B&B Italia
250 Brompton Road
London SW3 2AS
020 7591 8111
www.bebitalia.com
Contemporary furniture and lifestyle accessories.

Baileys Home
Whitecross Farm
Bridstow
Ross-on-Wye
Herefordshire HR9 6JU
01989 561931
www.baileyshome.com
Rustic and utilitarian homewares.

Christopher Jones Antiques
Core One, The Gasworks
2 Michael Road
London SW6 2AN
07775 900 436/438
www.christopherjonesantiques.co.uk
Interesting 18th-, 19th- and 20th-century decorative antiques.

Fontaine Decorative
The Old Laundry
St Johns Road
Margate
Kent CT9 1LU
01843 220 974
07855 360475
www.fontainedecorative.com
A unique and diverse selection of continental antiques.

Gubi
07769 992009
www.gubi.com
Reproduction furniture and lighting, retro-style.

Metro Retro
Seabrooks Farm
Church Lane
Little Leighs
Essex CM3 1PG
01245 363764
www.metroretro.co.uk
Vintage furniture from reclaimed materials.

Porta Romana
Design Centre Chelsea Harbour
Unit G8
London SW10 0XE
020 7352 0440
www.portaromana.co.uk
Furniture, lighting and accessories.

Spencer Swaffer Antiques
30 High Street
Arundel
West Sussex BN18 9AB
01903 882132
www.spencerswaffer.com
Italian and continental antiques, including garden furniture.

Villaverde Ltd
112 New Kings Road
London SW6 4LY
020 7384 1577
www.villaverdeltd.com
Custom Italian lighting and furniture.

KITCHENS

Alessi Shop
www.alessi.com
Online source for quirky Italian-designed kitchen accessories and electrical appliances.

Hendy's Home Store
36 High Street
Hastings
Kent TN34 3ER
01424 447 171
www.homestore-hastings.co.uk
Reclaimed hardware and homewares.

Labour & Wait
85 Redchurch Street,
London E2 7DJ
020 7729 6253
www.labourandwait.co.uk
Home accessories with a reclaimed or vintage aesthetic.

Smeg UK Ltd
3 Milton Park
Abingdon
Oxfordshire OX14 4RN
0844 557 0070
www.smeguk.com
Retro kitchen appliances.

BATHROOMS

Catchpole & Rye
Chelsea Walk
282–284 Fulham Road
London SW10 9EW
020 73510940
www.catchpoleandrye.com
Antique-style bathrooms.

TuttoBagno
www.tuttobagno.co.uk
*Contemporary bathrooms designed
and manufactured in Italy.*

TEXTILES &
WALLPAPERS

Dedar
Design Centre East Chelsea
Harbour
Unit C7
London SW10 0XF
020 7351 9939
www.dedar.com
*Fine Italian wallpapers and
fabrics from Milan.*

L'Officina dell'Invisibile
www.officinadellinvisibile.it
*Soft furnishings, lighting and
jewellery from Carlotta Odone
(see pages 18–23)*

Romo Ltd
Design Centre Chelsea
Harbour
Lots Road
London SW10 0XE
01623 750005
www.romo.com
Fabrics and wall coverings.

Rubelli
Design Centre East Chelsea
Harbour
Unit C9
London SW10 0XF
020 7349 1590
*A Venetian family company
specializing in both traditional
and contemporary designs.*

PAINTS & TILES

Paola Angoletta Interiors
paolaangoletta@gmail.com
*Custom paint effects and
restoration (see Paola's work in
her own home on pages 36–43).*

Bibliotheque
Unit 11 Devonshire Business
Centre
Cranborne Road
Potters Bar
Hertfordshire EN6 3JR
01707 649932
www.bibliotheque.co.uk
*Italian luxury porcelain tiles and
mosaics for walls and floors.*

Farrow & Ball
www.farrow-ball.com
*Wide range of unusual, chalky
hues and rich Italianate colours.*

LimeStone Gallery
583 King's Road
London SW6 2EH
020 7828 6900
www.limestonegallery.com
*Bespoke stonework in limestone,
marble, onyx and granite*

US SOURCES

ITALIAN ANTIQUES

Italian Antique Imports
561-635-1578
www.italianantiqueimports.com
*Online source for antique
furniture and architectural
supplies.*

Legacy Antiques
1406 Slocum St.
Dallas, TX 75207
www.legacyantiques.com
Italian and continental furniture.

Mercato Antiques
33071 W. 83rd Street
DeSoto, KS 66018
913-583-1511
www.mercatoantiques.com
*Direct importer for Italian
antiques, artifacts and tableware.*

Urban Chateau
www.urbanchateau.com
*Online source for fine European
antiques, including Italian pieces.*

SALVAGE &
RECLAMATION

Amighini Architectural
www.amighini.com
*Specialists in doors, antique tiles
and rustic furniture.*

Building REsources
701 Amador Street
San Francisco, CA 94124
415-285-7814
www.buildingresources.org
*Reusable, recycled and
re-manufactured building and
landscaping materials.*

The Demolition Depot
216 East 125th Street (between
2nd & 3rd Ave)
New York, NY 10035
212-860-1138
www.demolitiondepot.com
*Lamps and mirrors as well as
religious items.*

Heritage Salvage
1473 Petaluma Blvd South
Petaluma, California 94952
707-762-6277
www.heritagesalvage.com
Reclaimed building materials.

KITCHENS &
BATHROOMS

Bella Soleil
www.bellasoleil.com
*Online supplier of Italian pottery
and Deruta ceramics including
Maiolica dinnerware.*

Biordi Art Imports
412 Columbus Avenue
San Francisco, CA 94133
415-392-8096
www.biordi.com
*Museum-quality ceramics
including Italian dinnerware and
classic Maiolica.*

The Pottery Co.
The Willow
183 Water Street
Exeter, NH 03833
603-770-2968
www.thepotteryco.com
Italian tiles and ceramics.

Restoration Hardware
www.restorationhardware.com
*Vintage-style hardware and home
furnishings and accessories,
including lighting.*

Thatsarte.com
www.thatsarte.com
800-450-6170
*Online source for authentic
handmade maiolica.*

PAINTS & TILES

Italian Marble
1-866-860-1710
www.italianmarble.com
*Statuary, mosaics, fireplaces and
flooring.*

**The Old Fashioned Milk
Paint Co., Inc.**
436 Main Street
Groton, Massachusetts 01450
978-448-6336
*Authentic paints for historic
furniture and houses.*

TEXTILES

**Kathleen Taylor
The Lotus Collection**
445 Jackson Street
San Francisco, CA 94111
415-398-8115
www.ktaylor-lotus.com
*Antique European textiles,
tapestries and pillows.*

Schweitzer Linen
www.schweitzerlinen.com
Luxury Italian bed linens

Picture and Business Credits

Endpapers: Left-hand page, clockwise from bottom left: The home of Mariella Ienna in Palermo. Ph: Debi Treloar; Ph: Martin Brigdale; Designed by Viviana Haddad in association with Marta Tacchini. Ph: Debi Treloar; Ph: Debi Treloar; Ph: Debi Treloar; The home of Mariella Ienna in Palermo. Ph: Debi Treloar; A project by Marco Livadiotti. Photography by Alessandra Ianniello/Living Inside; Ph: Debi Treloar. Right-hand page, clockwise from bottom left: The home of Paola Angoletta, www.paolaangoletta.com. Ph: Stefano Scatà/The Interior Archive; Ph: Debi Treloar; The home of Mariella Ienna in Palermo. Ph: Debi Treloar; Ph: Debi Treloar; Ph: Ian Wallace; A project by Marco Livadiotti. Photography by Alessandra Ianniello/Living Inside; Ph: Debi Treloar; A project by Marco Livadiotti. Photography by Alessandra Ianniello/Living Inside. Pages 1–9 ph: Debi Treloar; 10–11 ph: Alan Williams; 12 below left ph: Alan Williams; 12 below right ph: Peter Cassidy; 12 centre right ph: Alan Williams; 12 above right ph: © Stephen Bisgrove/Alamy; 13 above left, above right, below right ph: Alan Williams; 13 centre right ph: © Ken Scicluna/JAI/Corbis; 14 background ph: Laura Edwards; 14 insert and 15 ph: Ian Wallace; 16–17 ph: © Unlisted Images/Corbis; 18–23 The apartment of Carlotta Oddone in Turin, Italy. Carlotta works between Turin and Rio de Janeiro, where she has opened a store with her brand. www.officinadellinvisibile.it. Ph: Fabrizio Cicconi/Living Inside. Styling by Francesca Davoli; 24 left ph: © BYphoto/Alamy; 24 centre ph: Martin Brigdale; 24 right ph: Peter Cassidy; 25 ph: Peter Cassidy apart from below right (ph: Martin Brigdale); 26 ph: Clare Winfield; 27 ph: Ian Wallace; 28–33 the home of Katrin Arens in Villa d'Adda, www.katrinarens.it. (Originally featured in *Recycled Home* by Mark and Sally Bailey, www.baileyshome.com). ph: Debi Treloar; 34 below left ph: © Stuart Franklin/Magnum Photos; 34 below right ph: © Bruno Barbey/Magnum Photos; 34 above right ph: © Robert Harding World Imagery/Alamy; 35 above © Moviestore collection Ltd/Alamy; 35 below Vanni and Nicoletta Calamai's home near Siena. Ph: Chris Tubbs; 36–43 The home of Paola Angoletta, www.paolaangoletta.com. Ph: Stefano Scatà/The Interior Archive; 44–45 ph: Martin Brigdale; 46 ph: Debi Treloar; 47 above left ph: Peter Cassidy; 47 above centre ph: Kate Whitaker; 47 above right ph: Peter Cassidy; 47 below right ph: Kate Whitaker; 47 below centre ph: Debi Treloar; 47 below left ph: Peter Cassidy; 48–57 The home of Pietro Castagna in Pescallo, Lake Como, www.castagna.info. For details of holiday rentals, please visit www.pescallo.com. Ph: Stefania Giorgi; 58 ph: William Reavell; 59 ph: Ian Wallace; 60–65 ph: Peter Cassidy; 66–71 Brogino is available to rent from Invitation to Tuscany, www.invitationtotuscany.co.uk. Ph: Chris Tubbs; 72 insert below left ph: Steve Painter; 72 insert below right ph: © Ian Berry/Magnum Photos; 73 above left ph: © Macduff Everton/Corbis; 73 above right ph: Steve Painter; 73 centre right ph: Jonathan Smith/Getty Images; 73 below ph: © Lars Halbauer/dpa/Corbis; 73 centre left ph: Steve Painter; 73 centre ph: Jean Cazals; 75 ph: Peter Cassidy; 76–83 Isabelle de Borchgrave. Architect : Jean-Philippe Gauvin. Ph: Chris Tubbs; 84 above Vanni and Nicoletta Calamai's home near Siena. Ph: Chris Tubbs; 84 below right Giorgio and Ilaria Miani's Podere Casellacce in Val d'Orcia. Ph: Chris Tubbs; 84 below centre Teresa Ginori's home near Varese. Ph: Chris Tubbs; 84 below left ph: Peter Cassidy; 85 above left ph: Vanni and Nicoletta Calamai's home near Siena. Ph: Chris Tubbs; 85 above right ph: Kate Whitaker; 85 below right ph: Peter Cassidy; 86–91 A house in Maremma, Tuscany designed by Contemporanea. Ph: Chris Tubbs; 92 ph: Ruth Brown/Getty Images; 93 above left ph: © Atlantide Phototravel/Corbis; 93 above centre ph: © Herbert Monheim/Arcaid/Corbis; 93 above right ph: Roberto Soncin Gerometta/Getty Images; 93 below right ph: © Jean-Pierre Lescourret/Corbis; 93 below left ph: Martin Child/Getty Images; 94–95 ph: Ian Wallace; 96 above right ph: Peter Cassidy; 96 centre © Guenter Rossenbach/Corbis; 96 below right ph: Peter Cassidy; 96 below left ph: Peter Cassidy; 97 above left ph: William Lingwood; 97 above right ph: © Hubert Stadler/Corbis; 97 below right ph: David Munns; 98–105 Simone de Looze's home in Tuscany, Le Porciglia. Ph: Chris Tubbs; 106–107 ph: Martin Brigdale; 108–109 Photography by Alessandra Ianniello/Living Inside; 110 above left ph: Riama-Pathe/The Kobal Collection; 110 above right ph: Cineriz/The Kobal Collection; 110 centre right ph: Titanus /SNPC/The Kobal Collection; 110 below right Cecchi Gori /TIGER/Canal +/The Kobal Collection; 110 below left ph: CCC/Cineriz/ FRANCINEX/TCF/The Kobal Collection; 110 centre left ph: Produzione De Sica/The Kobal Collection; 111 above CRISTALDIFILM/FILMS ARIANE/The Kobal Collection; 111 below Cino Del Duca/PCE/LYRE/ The Kobal Collection; 112–113 ph: Ian Wallace; 114–121 A project by Marco Livadiotti. Photography by Alessandra Ianniello/Living Inside; 122 insert ph: © Christine Webb/Alamy; 123 above left ph: Mel Watson/Getty Images; 123 above centre ph: Danita Delimont/Getty Images; 123 above right ph: Debi Treloar; 123 below right ph: De Agostini/A. Dagli Orti/Getty Images; 123 below left ph: Sebastian Abbado's "I Falchi" in Val d'Orcia. Ph: Chris Tubbs; 124–125 ph: Richard Jung; 126–133 The Rome apartment of interior designer Andrea Truglio. Ph: Debi Treloar; 134 above right ph: © Alfredo Dagli Orti/The Art Archive/Corbis; 134 centre ph: © David Seymour/Magnum Photos; 134 below ph:

© Ken Scicluna/JAI/Corbis; **135** above left ph: De Agostini/
A. Dagli Orti/Getty Images; **135** above right ph: ©
Ferdinando Scianna/Magnum Photos; **135** below left ph:
© Ferdinando Scianna/Magnum Photos; **135** centre left ph:
© Peter Scholey/Robert Harding World Imagery/Corbis;
136 ph: Peter Cassidy; page**137** ph: Martin Brigdale; **138–143**
designed by Marco Costanzi (www.marcocostanzi.com).
Ph: Max Zambelli; **144–145** ph: Debi Treloar; **146–147**
background ph: Peter Cassidy; **146** above left ph: Peter Cassidy;
146 above centre ph: Peter Cassidy; **146** above right ph: Kate
Whitaker; **146** below right ph: Peter Cassidy; **146** below
centre ph: Steve Painter; **146** below left ph: Peter Cassidy;
148 ph: Martin Brigdale; **149** ph: Peter Cassidy; **150–151** ph:
Debi Treloar; **153** ph: Ian Wallace; **154, 155, 157** and **159**
images courtesy of Luisa Beccaria, www.luisabeccaria.it;
156 and **158** ph: Simon Upton; **160–161** ph: Debi Treloar;
162 above right © Ian Nolan/Alamy; **162** below right ph:
Peter Cassidy; **162** below centre ph: © Owen Franken/Corbis;
162 below left ph: Richard Jung; **163** above left ph: © Alex
Segre/Alamy; **163** above right ph: Steve Baxter; **163** centre
right ph: Gus Filgate; **163** below right ph: © Ferdinando
Scianna/Magnum Photos; **163** centre left ph: © John
Angerson/Alamy; **164** ph: Clare Winfield; **165** ph: Martin
Brigdale; **166–175** The home of Velasco Vitali, designed by
Arturo Montanelli (www.arturomontanelli.com). All paintings
and sculptures © Velasco Vitali (www.velascovitali.com). Ph:
Debi Treloar; **176–177** background ph: Peter Cassidy; **177**
above left ph: Steve Painter; **177** above centre ph: Steve
Painter; **177** above right ph: © Bon Appetit/Alamy; **177** below
right ph: Jean Cazals; **177** below centre ph: © M.Flynn/Alamy;
177 below left ph: Jean Cazals; **179** ph: Martin Brigdale;
180–187 Designed by Viviana Haddad in association with
Marta Tacchini. Ph: Debi Treloar; **188–189** ph: Steve Painter;
188 above left ph: Debi Treloar; **188** above right ph: © Stuart
Freedman/In Pictures/Corbis; **188** centre right ph: ©
Matthew Williams-Ellis/ Robert Harding World
Imagery/Corbis; **188** below right ph: © BERTOLISSIO
Giovanni/Hemis/Corbis; **188** below left ph: © Robert
Harding World Imagery/ Alamy; **188** centre left ph: ©
Ferdinando Scianna/ Magnum Photos; **188** centre ph: © Tibor
Bognar/ Corbis; **189** insert ph: © Unlisted Images,
Inc./Alamy; **190** ph: Martin Brigdale; **191** ph: Peter Cassidy;
192–193 ph: Debi Treloar; **194–201** The home of Mariella
Ienna in Palermo. Ph: Debi Treloar; **202, 205** and **208** ph:
Debi Treloar.

BUSINESS CREDITS

Carlotta Oddone
www.officinadellinvisibile.it
Pages 18–23

Katrin Arens
info@katrinarens.it
www.katrinarens.it
Pages 28–33

Paola Angoletta
www.paolaangoletta.com
Pages 36–43

Pietro Castagna
www.castagna.info
www.pescallo.com
Pages 48–57

Brogino
www.invitationtotuscany.co.uk
Pages 66–71

**Werner and Isabelle de
  Borchgrave**
www.isabelledeborchgrave.com
and
Jean-Philippe Gauvin
  (architect)
www.gauvin-architectes.com
Pages 76–83

Anna Garcea
www.contemporanealondon.
  com
Pages 86–91

Simone de Looze
Simone de Looze Interiors
+39 335 5720685
Pages 98–103

Andrea Truglio
www.andreatruglio.com
Pages 126–133

Marco Costanzi
www.marcocostanzi.com
138–143

Luisa Beccaria
www.luisabeccaria.it
154–159

Velasco Vitali
www.velascovitali.com
and
Arturo Montanelli
www.arturomontanelli.com
Pages 166–175

Viviana Haddad
viviana.haddad72@gmail.com
www.viviana-haddad.com
Studio:
Via Exaudinos, 17–97015
  Modica (RG)
+39 339 6611369
Pages 180–187

Mariella Ienna
mariella.ienna.design@gmail.
  com
Paintings by:
www.moniqueloveringstudio.
  com
Pages 194–201

Index

Figures in italics indicate captions.

conscious of an inferiority.

Samuel Johnson

A man who has not
been in Italy is always
conscious of an inferiority.

Samuel Johnson